entering
CHRIST'S
prayer

Father Eric Jensen has gifted us with a wonderful way to enter more fully into the mystery of Jesus' prayer. In an easily readable style, along with short substantial comments, he accomplishes, through the written word, what a skillful director might do in leading one through a personally guided week of prayer.

Father Jensen's book will have many different practical uses. It can be used as a guide for daily prayer for over several months or for a more intensive week-long silent retreat, with or without, a personal prayer guide. Readers who are familiar with the *Spiritual Exercises of St. Ignatius* will find this book a useful instrument in keeping with its structures and dynamics. Those not familiar with the *Exercises* will discover in the book a gentle non-imposing way of understanding such dynamics. For persons who desire a less structured approach, this book can be used as a deepening instrument of *Lectio Divina*.

Above all, Father Jensen leads the reader into a very deep appreciation of both Testaments. His comments deftly make the connections with First Testament which was the background and understanding for Luke's authorship of his Gospel. Thus, without reading all the biblical references that scholars place in our bibles, Jensen's approach moves the reader into the heart of Jesus which was imbued with that record of his Father's revelation.

Jon Veltri, S.J.
Ignatian Spirituality expert and author of *Orientations*

A Retreat in 32 Meditations

entering
CHRIST'S
prayer

Eric Jensen, S.J.

ave maria press AmP notre dame, indiana

© 2007 by Eric Jensen, S.J.

Founded in 1865, Ave Maria Press is a ministry of the Indiana Province of Holy Cross.

www.avemariapress.com

ISBN-10 1-59471-134-8 ISBN-13 978-1-59471-134-3

Cover and text design by Katherine Coleman.

Printed and bound in the United States of America.

Library of Congress Cataloging-in-Publication Data

Jensen, Eric, SJ.
    Entering Christ's prayer : a retreat in 32 meditations / by Eric Jensen.
        p. cm.
    ISBN-13: 978-1-59471-134-3 (pbk.)
    ISBN-10: 1-59471-134-8 (pbk.)
  1. Lord's prayer—Prayers and devotions. I. Title.

    BV230.J43 2007
    248.3'2—dc22

                            2007027257

In memory of

Joy Nicholson,

mother and teacher,

1925-2002

CONTENTS

PREFACE

This little book grew out of an eight-day retreat I made recently at Madonna House in Combermere, Ontario. While there, I decided to follow a suggestion, offered to me many years ago by Father Francis Martin, who was then a member of the Madonna House Community, to take for my prayer material a single gospel or psalm. At that time I settled on Psalm 103. This time I decided to use the Gospel of Luke. In an introduction to this gospel in the *Jerusalem Bible*, some of the things that make Luke unique were touched upon, among them the way Luke so often shows Jesus at prayer. Four or five passages where Jesus prays were noted. However, as I began to go through the gospel, I discovered many other passages, including somewhere prayer is not mentioned but can be surmised— as when Jesus goes off to a deserted place to be by himself. I began to be excited by the way prayer seemed to suffuse the entire Gospel of Luke.

This was more than enough to persuade me that I should follow the inspiration and see where it led. I felt already that I was being drawn into prayer, and so the grace I sought throughout the retreat was *Draw Me into Your Prayer*. This put me in mind of the title of a book by fellow Jesuit David L. Fleming: *Draw Me into Your Friendship: The Spiritual Exercises—A Literal Translation and a Contemporary Reading* (The Institute of Jesuit Sources, St. Louis, Missouri, 1996), which was appropriate since the *Ignatian Exercises* always provide, if not a scaffold for my retreat, at least a certain structure for my retreat day's prayer. What was of immense help was the magisterial work on Luke by Joseph A. Fitzmyer, S.J. in *The Gospel According to Luke: A New Translation with Introduction and Commentary*, volumes 28 and 28A in the Anchor Bible Series (Doubleday & Company, Inc., Garden City, New York, 1981 and 1985 respectively). While what follows takes its form and substance from my personal prayer and reflection, much of the understanding and interpretation of Luke's Gospel comes from Father Fitzmyer's study. While I do not quote his words, I would like to acknowledge my debt to him here. The translation used throughout this work, however, is not Joseph Fitzmyer's but that of the *New Revised Standard Version*.

ERIC JENSEN, S.J.
Loyola House
Ignatius Jesuit Centre of Guelph, Ontario, Canada

INTRODUCTION

How can I become a person of prayer? Is there a way into prayer that will lead me to a deeper relationship with God? I was sometimes asked these questions during my sixteen years of parish ministry. Many people, in their struggles with family life, loneliness, or work, are searching for a spirituality that will provide a living contact with God in their daily life. At times they may actually sense God's presence or have an inner awareness of a silent invitation to attentiveness. Is there a way into this inner world? In our longing for God we may come to recognize in the scriptures evidence of God's longing to connect with us. There are many ways into prayer through the word of God, but the Gospel of Luke is especially helpful because it reveals something of Jesus' own inner life of prayer. Jesus himself is the way—the way into prayer.

Drawn Into Jesus' Inner Life

Jesus' inner life of prayer, as Luke presents it, seems to have been one of continual communion with God—that is, with the Father and in the Holy Spirit. This has been the goal of all the great spiritual masters: to achieve union with God in contemplation. This too is one of the goals of the *Spiritual Exercises* of Saint Ignatius Loyola, but the ultimate goal is to help us achieve the end for which we are created: the praise, reverence, and service of God (as expressed in the "Principle and Foundation," paragraph 23 in the text of the *Exercises*). This end is achieved through the following of Jesus in our daily life. But it is especially through contemplation of Jesus in the gospels that the disciple learns to "be like the teacher" (Lk 6:40). It is through this contemplation that we discover something of what following Jesus means. For Ignatius, with his great ideal of service, it seems to mean being a contemplative even in the midst of action—being like Jesus as he is depicted in the Gospel of Luke.

Meditation and Contemplation

Gospel contemplation, after the manner proposed by Ignatius in the *Spiritual Exercises*, calls for imagination. The kind of guided meditation given in my other book, *Who Is Jesus for Me?* (Novalis Press), is not contemplation in this sense. Ignatius does not guide one's images the way a facilitator guides them for a group in guided meditation. Instead he trusts that the Holy Spirit will guide each individual's images uniquely. Ignatius simply suggests the matter for prayer, specifying some details of the story (*historia*) in a "First Prelude." For instance, in the contemplation on the nativity of Jesus, he mentions Mary, about nine months pregnant, seated on a donkey, accompanied by Joseph and a maid, leading an ox (see paragraph 111 of the *Spiritual Exercises*). The ox and the donkey are details taken from paintings of the nativity, and are to be found, not in Luke's gospel, but in Isaiah 1:3 ("The ox knows its owner, and the donkey its master's crib; but Israel does not know, my people do not understand"). The actual imagining of the scene, however, is left to the one who is to contemplate it, who is asked "to see with the sight of the imagination the road from Nazareth to Bethlehem; considering the length and breadth, and whether such a road is level or through valleys or over hills; likewise looking at the place or cave of the Nativity, how large, how small, how low, how high, and how it was prepared" (paragraph 112).

Having imagined the setting in some concrete detail, one proceeds to imagine the persons, inserting oneself among them as a humble servant in order to attend to what these persons are saying and to consider what they are doing—and especially what Jesus is doing and for whom he does it: "and all this for me" (paragraph 116). The Incarnation and birth of Jesus present me with a profound mystery. By imagining for myself these moments in the life of Jesus, I allow myself to be drawn into the mystery that is Jesus himself. What Ignatius instructs me to ask for in these contemplations is "interior" or "internal" knowledge of Jesus. This has sometimes been rendered as "deep-felt" knowledge, but

it is more than this. It is knowledge of his mind and heart— "that I may more love and follow Him" (paragraph 104). Jesus is just about to be conceived in my prayer, and already Ignatius is focusing me on following him! Following Jesus— discipleship—is what these exercises are all about. Following him here and now, I will really come to know him as living and active in my life and in the world, but it is in contemplating Jesus in the gospels that I discover what is *involved* in following him. Having allowed the decisions and actions of his life to touch me deeply, I will be ready to commit my life to Jesus, to live as he did, out of love for him who loves me.

What is said here of the Incarnation and nativity can be applied to any gospel contemplation. By leaving us free to imagine the scene for ourselves, whatever it may be, Ignatius allows us to open ourselves to the inspiration of the Holy Spirit, who works in our contemplative imagining just as surely as in our meditative thinking, and can inspire amazing things when we enter whole-heartedly into this kind of prayer.

Desiring and Asking

Desire is the key to Ignatian prayer. Ignatius teaches the importance of asking for what one desires (and desiring what one asks for), since it is only by asking that we can verify that our prayer has been answered. At the beginning of each exercise, Ignatius tells us what to ask for. This varies and "has to be according to the subject matter" (paragraph 48) of each of the Four Weeks of the *Spiritual Exercises*. In the First Week, the chief grace is what Ignatius calls confusion, by which he means amazement that, despite my sinfulness, I am still greatly loved by God. In the other weeks, it is what he calls internal knowledge of Jesus (or knowledge of what he knows and feels), to grieve with him in his grieving and to rejoice with him in his rejoicing. And so, at the beginning of each contemplation, I suggest a particular grace to ask for—some aspect of Jesus' interiority into which you may desire to be drawn, so that you can be taught to see through his eyes and learn to pray with his heart.

Review of Prayer

Ignatius also teaches the importance of reflecting on our daily experience, including our experience of prayer. And so at the end of each contemplation, I suggest a time for *reviewing* the prayer while it is still fresh—not to remake the prayer, but to verify how the grace has been given, and to see what might be significant moments in the *experience* of praying, moments worth returning to and deepening in subsequent prayer. The prayer itself is the imaginative contemplating of a scene from the Gospel of Luke, entering into it in a way that leads gradually to conversation— to communication with Jesus, in speech, "as one friend speaks to another" (paragraph 54), or in silence, where the deepest communion occurs.

Interior Movements and Repetition

When we pray (especially then, though not only then), our spirit is being engaged and influenced by the Holy Spirit. We are also open to contrary influences, and so there are usually *interior movements* stirring in the depths of our being, which are the effects or signs of both these influences. Sometimes the movements are quite strong, but at other times they are very subtle and almost imperceptible. Thus, a ten-minute or fifteen-minute review (not of the gospel passage but of these interior movements during our prayer) allows us to reflect quietly on our *experience* of praying, and then make note of these movements and of how they moved us. It is to these notes that we turn in our *repetitions*, not to remake the entire prayer or try to do it better, but only to seek out those effect-bearing words or phrases, thoughts or images, that moved us in some way—that opened our eyes a little to see something new or that touched our hearts with a twinge of pain or the possibility of renewed hope.

Consolation, Desolation, and Discernment

When we say that something *moved* us, we are talking about feelings. However, when Ignatius talks about interior *movements* or *motions* in a person, he is talking not about feelings but about the *direction* in which our feelings are taking us, that is, either *toward* God or *away from* God. Feelings may be pleasant or painful, and *both* kinds of feelings can lead us either toward or away from God. The same can be said of our thoughts, images, fantasies, desires, decisions, and actions: they can draw us to or away from God.

Pleasant feelings can draw me toward God by kindling my love for Jesus or my joy in his presence. This interior movement *toward God* Ignatius would call *spiritual consolation* (paragraph 316). But it is also possible to get trapped in pleasant or pious feelings, to become complacent in them or subtly proud of myself for having them. This interior movement, arising out of pleasant feelings but leading me *away from God* and turning me in on myself, Ignatius would call *spiritual desolation* (paragraph 317).

Painful feelings can also draw me to God by deepening my sorrow for sin or my distress at Jesus' death on the cross. This may not *feel* like consolation, but it *is* spiritual consolation, because its direction is *toward God*. Painful feelings such as discouragement, self-pity, or despair can imprison me in myself and, through loss of hope, lead me away from God. This interior movement is recognized as *spiritual desolation* because of its direction. The more important thing is not the feeling itself, but the *direction* of its movement *to* or *away from* God. Consolation and desolation are therefore understood by Ignatius to be spiritual experiences—the result of the powerful or subtle influence of good and evil spirits, that is, of the Holy Spirit and of what Ignatius often calls "the enemy of our human nature." Because consolation is contrary to desolation, the *thoughts* that come from consolation are contrary to those that come from desolation (paragraph 317). Discernment of spirits is the attending to our inner experience—our feelings especially, in order to distinguish the direction of their movement, and also our thoughts, in order to determine whether they lead us to or away from God.

When our focus is on Jesus or on the working of the Trinity in our lives, we grow in the virtues of hope, faith, and love, and we experience spiritual consolation. When we are isolated and turned in on ourselves, we lose hope, we begin to doubt, and we find it harder to love others or to love ourselves or to love God: this is an experience of spiritual desolation. The order—*hope*, faith, and love (paragraph 316)—is not always preserved in every translation of the *Exercises*, but it is significant that, in the original text, hope is mentioned first: the slide into desolation often begins with an eroding of hope. In a similar way, restoration of consolation frequently has its beginning in a renewal of hope, which in turn leads to renewed faith and renewed love.

The Rhythm of Prayer

If one is praying one hour a day, the rhythm of prayer unfolds in the course of the week. On retreat, when one is praying four or five times a day, prayer takes on a certain rhythm with the structuring of the day. The structure I used in this retreat was simply to pray four times a day, for an hour each time, making use of passages from the gospel for the first two prayer periods, and doing what Ignatius calls a *repetition* in the third period and an *application of the senses* in the fourth. Repetition involves going back to something, but what is gone back to is only a small part of the original prayer experience. Repetition involves going over something again, but what is gone over in the third prayer period is only what may seem to provide an avenue for going deeper into the experience. Since the interior movements that we are going back to may not be all that evident to begin with, there is a kind of discerning in both the review of prayer and the repetition, a searching for something only dimly seen or vaguely felt, if seen or felt at all. And so we pray, asking to have our eyes opened and our awareness heightened.

The *application of the senses* can only be understood analogously as referring to *spiritual* senses. When Psalm 34:8 exclaims, "O Taste and see that the Lord is good," it can hardly refer to a physical tasting or seeing. And yet we know at once what is meant: a certain savoring of an experience of God's goodness, an awareness or recognition of the loving-kindness of God. Prayer is also taken up with the sense of listening: "Speak, Lord, for your servant is listening" (1 Sm 4:9), and with being attentive to what the Spirit is doing in us. As well, we often talk of being touched by something in prayer or of "touching into" something. The risen Jesus says to the disciples, "See that it is I myself; touch me and see" (Lk 24:39). We can see and touch Jesus in imaginative and loving contemplation. Besides taste and sight, listening and touching, the sense of smell is especially associated with prayer, which is compared with the fragrance of incense: "Let my prayer be counted as incense before you, and the lifting up of my hands as an evening sacrifice" (Ps 141:2). In the same way, the golden bowls of incense in Revelation 5:8 symbolize "the prayers of the saints" on earth, rising like fragrant smoke to heaven.

Having already gone back (in the repetition) to deepen some part of our experience of God at work in our praying, we go back yet again (in the application of the senses) to savor the experience. In this kind of prayer, our minds are not engaged in trying to understand something. Rather, the deepest part of our being is simply resting in a "Presence," and, if any words are uttered, they are few. Our prayer takes on the rhythm of a continuing conversation. If prayer can be experienced as a loving conversation extending over the course of a day, then we can understand that, as the day comes to its close, there is less and less need to speak. It is enough simply to be in the presence of the "Other," reflecting quietly on all that has transpired between us and allowing one's heart to expand with gratitude and love.

A Unique Relationship

Each of us is unique, and to each of us God relates uniquely. What Ignatius provides is not a straitjacket for prayer but a very simple way of entering into this unique relationship with the Trinity and in particular with Jesus, who knows us and loves us just as we are, and who desires to be better known and more deeply loved by us. It is in reading and praying the gospels that we come to know Jesus, and to love him in such a way that we will go beyond praying into following. It is in struggling to follow Jesus that we really get to know him. The movement from knowing to loving to following, to new knowing and greater loving and closer following, is more than a circular one. It spirals upward in an ascent that draws us not only into Jesus' prayer but eventually into the embrace of the Triune God. The Gospel of Luke really *is* suffused with prayer, but, in the prayer of Jesus, there is a dynamic movement drawing him deeper and deeper into the love of God, a love which is already at work in him through the Spirit, a love leading to complete surrender to and total union with the One he calls Father. It is this dynamic movement that we enter into when we pray this gospel with Jesus and in the Spirit.

In entering into this dynamic movement we come to realize that it is not so much we who are inviting God into our prayer, but rather it is Jesus who is inviting us into God's prayer, into his own endless, loving conversation with the Father in the Spirit, a conversation filled with concern and compassion for us and for the whole of creation.

There's plenty of room for adapting what is offered in the pages that follow. What I have *not* done is provide the text or summary of an actual contemplation. Instead I have given brief introductions to the scripture passages, highlighting what I have found helpful for entering into this kind of prayer. There are eight chapters, each with four contemplations. They aren't meant to be read through mechanically—one can pick and choose. These thirty-two possibilities for prayer should be taken slowly, making use of Ignatius' simple techniques of repetition and application of the senses so as to deepen the affective experience in the prayer periods that follow. The eight chapters lend themselves to a retreat of eight day, but for use in daily life the material could be extended over several months. However you use these texts, you will discover that the Gospel of Luke offers a way into the mind and heart of Jesus through his prayer. Whether it is our own mind that is first engaged or our imagination, the important thing is that we allow our heart to be engaged—that we allow ourselves to enter into loving and being loved—as we are drawn into a simple and intimate dialogue, and eventually into surrender and silence.

BEFORE YOU BEGIN

It may be helpful to clarify our understanding of what Luke is attempting to do in his gospel, and especially in his infancy narrative, before contemplating the material he gives us.

What Is a Gospel?

The gospels are not biography or history in the ordinary sense of the word, though they contain much that is historical and factual. Each gospel is a final stage in a process that began with Jesus' ministry of teaching and healing, that continued with the Apostles' proclamation of the good news about Jesus' death and resurrection, and that concluded with an attempt to preserve in writing something of this apostolic proclamation.

The Gospel According to Luke

Luke begins his gospel by saying that "many have undertaken to set down an orderly account of the events that have been fulfilled among us, just as they were handed on to us by those who were eye-witnesses and servants of the word" (1:1-2). He too is attempting to do this (1:3), and so he claims to be writing as a historian, and yet what he is writing is not history but gospel—a unique literary form distinct from that of historical narrative. Still, he presents Jesus as a thoroughly historical personage, fully human and fully involved in the concrete, historical reality of his day.

Luke's Story of the Childhood of Jesus

The infancy narratives (found only in Matthew and Luke) are somewhat similar to the pre-history we find in the first eleven chapters of the Book of Genesis: they deal with beginnings, with origins, and they involve a re-interpretation of ancient texts rather than an account of what may actually have happened. They are an imaginative re-creation on the part of both Matthew and Luke, and praying these texts calls for an imaginative re-creation on our part.

A Story Embedded in History

While Luke's infancy narrative may be an imaginative re-creation, it nonetheless presents Jesus' conception and birth as taking place in history, connecting him with John the Baptist, situating both John and Jesus "in the days of King Herod of Judea" (1:5) and in the larger context of the Roman Empire and Emperor Augustus (2:1).

The Gospel of Jesus Versus the Gospel of Caesar

The angel who announces to shepherds the birth of a divine savior, proclaims it as "good news of great joy for all the people"—in the *New Revised Standard Version* (2:10). Literally, the text reads, "I *evangelize* to you great joy." Luke does not actually use the noun for *good news* or *gospel* but only the verb, yet (and on this point I depart from Joseph Fitzmyer's interpretation) it would seem to be implied. The

Greek word for *good news* or *gospel* (*euangelion*) was associated in the Roman Empire at that time with Caesar Augustus, who was proclaimed a divine savior of the whole world. But here the *Savior* is not Augustus but Jesus, whose other titles are *Messiah* and *Lord*—*Lord* being the title of divinity (2:11). These three titles place Jesus, the true divine savior and king, in opposition to the emperor. They proclaim a gospel of true peace (2:14) in opposition to the gospel of Caesar with its *Pax Romana* imposed by military might. Finally, they set the stage for the coming Crucifixion of Jesus, as well as for the persecution of his followers, which Luke will recount in his second volume, the Acts of the Apostles.

A Story Embedded in Prayer

Luke puts all this also in the context of prayer, as we will see. It is this context of prayer that we want to consider.

I.

JESUS' HIDDEN LIFE OF PRAYER

Read the preparatory material below and choose two of the following passages for today's prayer.

A. *Conceived in Prayer:*

   The Mystery of His Incarnation

   Luke 1:26–56

B. *Born Into Prayer:*

   The Mystery of His Birth

   Luke 2:1–19

C. *Surrounded by Prayer:*

   The Mystery of His Naming and Presentation

   Luke 2:21–40

D. *Growing in Prayer:*

   The Mystery of His Calling

   Luke 2:41–52

It is impossible to think of the hidden life of Jesus—the childhood, adolescence, and young adulthood spent in Nazareth—without thinking also of his prayer.

BACKGROUND

A Tradition of Pious Prayer

Jesus would have shared in the rich tradition of piety that shaped the life of the people of Israel, in the home, in the synagogue, and in the temple. Luke's infancy narrative, found in the first two chapters of his gospel, shows us something of this piety in his stories of Mary and Joseph, Elizabeth and Zechariah, Simeon and Anna.

A Doubly Hidden Life of Prayer

Because the first thirty years or so of Jesus' life are hidden, in the sense that there is no historical account of them, we can say that his prayer life is also hidden. Furthermore, since his prayer was not just public and liturgical but also interior and private, we can say that it is doubly hidden.

An Imagined Life of Prayer

What might Jesus' interior life of prayer have been like? We cannot know, but we can try to imagine it in our reading and praying of this gospel. Praying the hidden life of Jesus may seem to present a difficulty, since Luke provides so little information about this part of his life, and what information *is* provided in the first two chapters is of a different sort from that found in what follows them.

A Story Unfolding in Prayer

The announcement of the Baptist's birth is made in the Temple of Jerusalem during a time of worship and public prayer: "Now at the time of the incense offering, the whole assembly of the people was praying outside" (1:10). Zechariah is presented not only as a priest but also as a man of prayer, whose prayer has been heard and whose wife Elizabeth will bear him a son (1:13). Thus, from the very first chapter, this gospel takes up the theme of prayer that will run throughout, and prayer will again be mentioned explicitly toward the end of this infancy narrative, when Anna makes her appearance in the story (2:36–38).

A Story for Contemplation

When we ourselves attempt to contemplate the story of Jesus' conception, birth, and boyhood in our own prayer, we might take Luke himself as our guide and do what he did: we can make prayer the context in which we set the scenes that follow, and make explicit what may be only implicit (if that) in these passages.

Before You Pray

1. Read the gospel passage slowly and carefully, seeking to understand it more deeply in its totality or in its parts as you wish.

2. Read the section Exploring the Gospel as an aid both to understanding the text and to stimulating your imagination when you pray.

3. Before you begin to pray, read the passage once again.

A. CONCEIVED IN PRAYER: THE MYSTERY OF HIS INCARNATION

LUKE 1:26–56

In the sixth month the angel Gabriel was sent by God to a town in Galilee called Nazareth, to a virgin engaged to a man whose name was Joseph, of the house of David. The virgin's name was Mary. (1:26–27)

And he came to her and said, "Greetings, favored one! The Lord is with you." But she was much perplexed by his words and pondered what sort of greeting this might be. The angel said to her, "Do not be afraid, Mary, for you have found favor with God. And now you will conceive in your womb and bear a son, and you will name him Jesus. He will be great, and will be called the Son of the Most High, and the Lord God will give him the throne of his ancestor David. He will reign over the house of Jacob forever, and of his kingdom there will be no end." Mary said to the angel, "How can this be, since I am a virgin?" The angel said to her, "The Holy Spirit will come upon you, and the power of the Most High will overshadow you; therefore the child to be born will be holy; he will be called the Son of God. And now, your relative Elizabeth in her old age has also conceived a son; and this is the sixth month for her who was said to be barren. For nothing will be impossible with God." (28–37)

Then Mary said, "Here am I, the servant of the Lord; let it be with me according to your word." Then the angel departed from her. (38)

In those days Mary set out and went with haste to a Judean town in the hill country, where she entered the house of Zechariah and greeted Elizabeth. When Elizabeth heard Mary's greeting, the child leaped in her womb. And Elizabeth was filled with the Holy Spirit and exclaimed with a loud cry, "Blessed are you among women, and blessed is the fruit of your womb. And why has this happened to me, that the mother of my Lord comes to me? For as soon as I heard the sound of your greeting, the child in my womb leaped for joy. And blessed is she who believed that there would be a fulfillment of what was spoken to her by the Lord." (39–45)

And Mary said,

"My soul magnifies the Lord, and my spirit rejoices in God my savior,

for he has looked with favor on the lowliness of his servant.

Surely, from now on all generations will call me blessed,

for the Mighty One has done great things for me,

and holy is his name.

His mercy is for those who fear him from generation to generation.

He has shown strength with his arm;

he has scattered the proud in the thoughts of their hearts.

He has brought down the powerful from their thrones,

and lifted up the lowly.

He has filled the hungry with good things, and sent the rich away empty.

He has helped his servant Israel, in remembrance of his mercy,

according to the promise he made to our ancestors,

to Abraham and to his descendants forever." (46–55)

And Mary remained with her about three months and then returned to her home. (56)

THE HOLY SPIRIT WILL COME UPON YOU, AND THE POWER OF THE MOST HIGH WILL OVERSHADOW YOU; THEREFORE THE CHILD TO BE BORN WILL BE HOLY; HE WILL BE CALLED THE SON OF GOD.

EXPLORING THE GOSPEL

The Incarnation

In the *Spiritual Exercises*, Ignatius puts the story of Luke's annunciation at the back of the book, among various other texts, which can be suggested by a director. He begins the second week of the *Exercises* instead with an imaginative creation of his own. There the contemplation on the Incarnation (paragraphs 101–109) invites us to see how the Three Divine Persons of the Trinity look with compassion on "all the earth" and decree that the Second Person should become a human being to save the human race (paragraph 102). This gives the Incarnation a cosmic dimension, placing its motive in the compassionate love of the Triune God, who is intimately involved in the unfolding of creation.

Was Mary Also Praying?

Luke presents the story of the origin of John the Baptist in an imaginatively constructed scene in which both Elizabeth and Zechariah are described as "righteous before God, living blamelessly" (1:6). The angel appears to Zechariah in the sanctuary while "the whole assembly of the people was praying outside" (1:10), with John's conception coming as an answer to prayer (1:13). Since the announcement of Jesus' conception is made to Mary in this same first chapter of Luke's gospel, it seems appropriate to extend this context of prayer to her as well.

ENTERING INTO CONTEMPLATION

1. CHOOSE WHERE YOU WILL PRAY
   COMPOSE YOURSELF FOR PRAYER

Find a quiet place where you can be alone and uninterrupted for an hour. Take time to be still, to be present to God, and to express both your longing to know the mind and heart of Jesus and your desire to follow him more faithfully in your daily life.

2. IMAGINE THE SCENE

In his *Spiritual Exercises,* Ignatius always invites us to imagine the scene for ourselves. And so, try to imagine Mary in some particular setting—a room in a house or a garden outside. Try to make it as detailed as it needs to be in order to have it come alive for you. But try also to imagine Mary at prayer, so that her conversation with the heavenly messenger (whom Luke introduces to us as Gabriel) becomes part of her communing with God.

3. ASK FOR THIS GRACE

Jesus, draw me into the mystery of your origin and Incarnation.

4. LISTEN TO WHAT THE PERSONS SAY

Though the exchange between Gabriel and Mary can be thought of as a wholly internal event, it is the purpose of scripture to make audible for us what cannot be heard, and to make visible what cannot be seen. You are privileged, in your imaginative prayer, to be part of this event. Try to attend to every precious word.

5. ENTER INTO CONVERSATION

When the angel departs (at the end of verse 38), you could imagine Mary remaining in this setting, amazed and very still. You could gaze on her as she continues her prayer in a new way and with a new awareness. She is conscious that something has happened in her, conscious that there is a new and marvelous presence within her, and is trying to understand what she has just experienced as she reflects upon it. At some point you may even try to speak with her, if you feel prompted to do so, though you may also hesitate to intrude in a moment that is so sacred and intimate and private.

IN THE SIXTH MONTH THE ANGEL GABBRIEL WAS SENT BY GOD TO A TOWN IN GALILEE CALLED NAZARETH, TO A VIRGIN ENGAGED TO A MAN WHOSE NAME WAS JOSEPH, OF THE HOUSE OF DAVID. THE VIRGIN'S NAME WAS MARY.

What to Pray on Next

You could do a second contemplation on one of the following passages (B, C, or D) before moving into a repetition of your first two prayer periods. Or, if your contemplation leads you to follow Mary on her journey to visit Elizabeth, you might try to imagine the long and arduous uphill trek from Nazareth to Jerusalem, and consider how she would travel—perhaps in the company of relatives or friends. You could even insert yourself in this company.

6. ENTER INTO SILENCE

It may be enough just to enter into Mary's stillness as she sits there. Sit there with her, and be present to her.

7. CONCLUSION

Thank Jesus for all that you have experienced in this prayer.

AFTER PRAYING

1. REFLECT ON THE EXPERIENCE

At the end of your contemplation, move to another place and spend a few minutes reviewing your experience of prayer, making note of those things that brought you either consolation or desolation, so that, if you do a repetition or application of the senses, you can return to them again, and enter more deeply into the mystery you are contemplating.

2. QUESTIONS THAT MAY ARISE OUT OF PRAYER

In your experience of contemplating Mary, was her prayer focused on God the Father? On the Holy Spirit? On the Son in her womb? On all three?

In contemplating Mary's visit to Elizabeth, what did you feel impelled her to go? Elizabeth's need for her help? Mary's desire to share her own experience? In moving into action, did Mary continue to be contemplative? Did she remain conscious of the presence within? Is this kind of awareness possible also for you?

3. SEARCHING THE SCRIPTURES

You may want to reflect on the account of Samuel's conception and birth, which Luke draws upon in his story of the origins of both John the Baptist and Jesus (1 Sm 1:1–2:11).

B. BORN INTO PRAYER: THE MYSTERY OF HIS BIRTH

LUKE 2:1–19

In those days a decree went out from Emperor Augustus that all the world should be registered. This was the first registration and was taken while Quirinius was governor of Syria. All went to their own towns to be registered. Joseph also went from the town of Nazareth in Galilee to Judea, to the city of David called Bethlehem, because he was descended from the house and family of David. He went to be registered with Mary, to whom he was engaged and who was expecting a child. While they were there, the time came for her to deliver her child. And she gave birth to her firstborn son and wrapped him in bands of cloth, and laid him in a manger, because there was no room for them in the inn. (2:1–7)

In that region there were shepherds living in the fields, keeping watch over their flock by night. Then an angel of the Lord stood before them, and the glory of the Lord shone around them, and they were terrified. But the angel said to them, "Do not be afraid, for see—I am bringing you good news of great joy for all the people: to you is born this day in the city of David a Savior, who is the Messiah, the Lord. This will be a sign for you: you will find a child wrapped in bands of cloth and lying in a manger." (8–12)

Before You Pray

1. Read the gospel passage slowly and carefully, seeking to understand it more deeply in its totality or in its parts as you wish.

2. Read the section Exploring the Gospel as an aid both to understanding the text and to stimulating your imagination when you pray.

3. Before you begin to pray, read the passage once again.

And suddenly there was with the angel a multitude of the heavenly host, praising God and saying, "Glory to God in the highest heaven, and on earth peace among those whom he favors." (13–14)

When the angels had left them and gone into heaven, the shepherds said to one another, "Let us go now to Bethlehem and see this thing that has taken place, which the Lord has made known to us." So they went with haste and found Mary and Joseph, and the child lying in the manger. When they saw this they made known what had been told them about this child; and all who heard it were amazed at what the shepherds told them. But Mary treasured all these words and pondered them in her heart. (15–19)

EXPLORING THE GOSPEL

What Can Artists Teach Us?

Contemplating the birth of Jesus may seem a lot like contemplating the scene on a Christmas card, or like contemplating a painting by an old master. But there is something we can learn from these pictures, and that is, *how artists have made use of both testaments to fashion a pictorial statement* and thus deepen our understanding of what is happening (and will happen) to Jesus.

Why the Ox and the Donkey?

Depictions of the birth of Jesus almost always include an ox and a donkey. Ignatius himself, in setting this scene for our contemplation, mentions Mary seated on a donkey "accompanied by Joseph and a maid, taking an ox, to go to Bethlehem" (*Spiritual Exercises*, paragraph 111). The maid is Ignatius' invention, but the ox and the donkey are an allusion to the First (or Old) Testament. An *allusion*, in writing or speaking, is usually a reference to something in history or in literature. The allusion here in Luke 2:7 (the allusive word is *manger* or *crib*) is to Isaiah 1:3, "The ox knows its owner, and the donkey its master's crib; but Israel does not know, my people

THIS WILL BE A SIGN FOR YOU: YOU WILL FIND A CHILD WRAPPED IN BANDS OF CLOTH AND LYING IN A MANGER.

do not understand." Painters turned this literary allusion into a pictorial one, directing our attention to this text of Isaiah, and implying that Jesus will not be understood or accepted. The ox and the donkey, however, have become so identified with the Christmas story that the allusion to Isaiah is often lost.

Putting Yourself in the Picture

Luke's first two chapters are a tissue of allusions to the First (or Old) Testament, the clearest being the allusion to Hannah's hymn of praise (1 Sm 2:1–10) in Mary's *Magnificat* (which takes its title from the opening word of the Latin translation, "*Magnificat anima mea Dominum*"). The bands of cloth enwrapping Jesus allude to the birth of David's son Solomon, who was royally swaddled this way (Wis 7:4–5). Many bibles list such allusions in notes, either at the foot of the page or down the side. When we contemplate this story and try to imagine it unfolding, we also do something creative when we insert our self in the scene, just as artists at one time would add their patron to the figures in their nativity paintings—and sometimes even include a self-portrait by way of a signature. Taking his cue from the old masters, Alfred Hitchcock, like artists in another medium, included himself unobtrusively in many of his films.

Revealing the Meaning of Events

Once we recognize the pictorial allusion in paintings of the birth of Jesus, we understand immediately that the artist (like Luke himself) is not simply trying to give us a historical representation of what may actually have happened, but is doing something more. The artist is telling us the *meaning* of what happened at Jesus' birth, while at the same time foreshadowing what will happen to him later when he begins his mission to Israel: for the most part, Jesus will not be understood, not even by his disciples. In a similar way, Luke is not giving us a historical account of what happened, but is directing our attention to ancient biblical events in order to underline the *meaning* of what is happening.

AND SHE GAVE BIRTH TO HER FIRSTBORN SON AND WRAPPED HIM IN BANDS OF CLOTH, AND LAID HIM IN A MANGER, BECAUSE THERE WAS NO ROOM FOR THEM IN THE INN.

Joseph also went from the town of Nazareth in Galilee to Judea, to the city of David called Bethlehem, because he was descended from the house and family of David.

Ushering in the Kingdom

What is the meaning behind these events? The meaning is revealed as parallel to that of the events in 1 Samuel 1 and 2: just as the miraculous birth of Hannah's son Samuel ushered in the beginning of the Kingdom of Israel, so also the birth of John the Baptist and the birth of Jesus usher in the beginning of a new kingdom. Looking ahead to Jesus' baptism, we see that, as Samuel was there to anoint David as king (and "the spirit of the Lord came mightily upon David from that day forward"—1 Samuel 16:13), so John the Baptist will be there at Jesus' anointing with the Holy Spirit (Lk 3:22).

Oppressing the People of Israel

The decree of Caesar (or Emperor) Augustus for a census, or registration of the population, provides a motive for Mary and Joseph to journey to Bethlehem (in the hills south of Jerusalem), where biblical tradition held that the Messiah would be born. This is a long and difficult uphill journey from Nazareth, but exactly how you imagine it is for you to decide. Bethlehem is the city of David's origin and of his first anointing, and so in Bethlehem we are again brought back to the beginnings of the Kingdom of Israel. The census demanded by Augustus (mainly for the oppressive purpose of taxation) reminds us of the census taken by David in 2 Samuel 24:1–17 (for the unpopular purpose of raising an army), where this is seen as something wicked and displeasing to God (and no doubt resented by the people). Though Luke is probably writing for predominantly gentile Christians outside of Palestine, we can imagine how this mention of a census would have been read by any inhabitant of the eastern empire, Gentile or Jew, who had lived under Rome's oppressive rule.

ENTERING INTO CONTEMPLATION

1. CHOOSE WHERE YOU WILL PRAY
   COMPOSE YOURSELF FOR PRAYER

Find a quiet place where you can be alone and uninterrupted for an hour. Take time to be still, to be present to God, and to express both your longing to know the mind and heart of Jesus and your desire to follow him more faithfully in your daily life.

2. IMAGINE THE SCENE

If you want to insert yourself in the scene, you might see yourself there not just as a servant but also as a child, one who has traveled with Mary and Joseph from Nazareth, or as one of the local children who has offered to assist them. This is one way of trying to receive the kingdom (and the king) as a little child (Lk 18:17). In contemplating Luke's nativity scene, it is important that you not feel yourself lost in the sweep of history but that you see yourself as known and loved from the beginning, as drawn into the compassion of God, and into the mystery of Jesus' birth in a suffering world.

3. ASK FOR THIS GRACE

Jesus, draw me into the mystery of your birth.

4. LISTEN TO WHAT THE PERSONS SAY

Luke gives us the words of the angel to the shepherd, announcing the birth of Jesus, but he does not give us any of the conversation between Mary and Joseph on their long and arduous journey to Bethlehem. You could try to imagine some of this: listen not only to what they say but also to how they say it. You might even try to imagine Mary's prayer during her labor, and Joseph's prayer also, as they turn to God for help in their time of need.

WHILE THEY WERE THERE, THE TIME CAME FOR HER TO DELIVER HER CHILD.

AND SUDDENLY THERE WAS WITH THE ANGEL A MULTITUDE OF THE HEAVENLY HOST, PRAISING GOD AND SAYING, "GLORY TO GOD IN THE HIGHEST HEAVEN, AND ON EARTH PEACE AMONG THOSE WHOM HE FAVORS."

5. ENTER INTO CONVERSATION

If you have traveled with Mary and Joseph all the way to Bethlehem, you already have a familiar relationship with them. You are there to help in whatever way you can. What do they ask you to do? How do they speak to you? How intimately do they invite you to share in their joy at Jesus' birth? Do they let you hold the newborn baby? What do you say to Jesus?

6. ENTER INTO SILENCE

The shepherds then visit this newborn infant, and relay the gospel message to his parents, who are simply amazed by it. "But Mary treasured all these words and pondered them in her heart" (2:19), meditating on their meaning. The scene concludes with more prayer, as the shepherds depart, "glorifying and praising God" (2:20). You may find yourself drawn into Mary's prayer, or into the praises of the angels.

7. CONCLUSION

Thank Jesus for all that you have received in this prayer.

AFTER PRAYING

1. REFLECT ON THE EXPERIENCE

At the end of your contemplation, move to another place and spend a few minutes reviewing your experience of prayer, making note of those things that brought you either consolation or desolation, so that, if you do a repetition or application of the senses, you can return to them again, and enter more deeply into the mystery you are contemplating.

2. QUESTIONS THAT MAY ARISE OUT OF PRAYER

In your experience of contemplating the birth of Jesus, what touched you most deeply? Recalling that, in Matthew's gospel (which Luke seems to have known), Jesus is born in a house

(2:11), why do you think Luke has Jesus born in what seems to be some sort of stall for donkeys or cattle? Does it bring out his desire to be identified with the poorest of the poor?

3. SEARCHING THE SCRIPTURES

Having contemplated Luke's nativity scene, it would perhaps be good to read through the story as Matthew presents it in 1:18–25. His chapter 2 is devoted to the story of the wise men (or magi) and King Herod. Matthew draws on different texts, especially from the book of Genesis, to reveal who Jesus is. His opening words in Greek may be translated literally as "Book of Genesis of Jesus Christ" (1:1). Matthew's Joseph twice receives a revelation in a dream, and takes Mary and Jesus to Egypt, recalling Joseph the dreamer (Gn 37:5–11, 19), who brought his family down to Egypt to preserve their life (Gn 46). Or you may want to read about the birth of Solomon, the son of David, in 2 Samuel 12:23–25, and in the Wisdom of Solomon, 7:1–6. Paul's hymn of praise to the humility of God, in Philippians 2:5–11, invites you to put on the mind and heart of Christ, who has become flesh for you, that you may love him more deeply and follow him more closely (see paragraph 104 in the *Spiritual Exercises*).

What to Pray on Next

If you have already contemplated the Incarnation and the birth of Jesus (sections A and B), then deepen the experience in a repetition and an application of senses. Otherwise go on to one of the passages in sections C or D.

Before You Pray

1. Read the gospel passage slowly and carefully, seeking to understand it more deeply in its totality or in its parts as you wish.

2. Read the section Exploring the Gospel as an aid both to understanding the text and to stimulating your imagination when you pray.

3. Before you begin to pray, read the passage once again.

C. SURROUNDED BY PRAYER: THE MYSTERY OF HIS NAMING AND PRESENTATION

LUKE 2:21–40

After eight days had passed, it was time to circumcise the child; and he was called Jesus, the name given by the angel before he was conceived in the womb. (21)

When the time came for their purification according to the law of Moses, they brought him up to Jerusalem to present him to the Lord (as it is written in the law of the Lord, "Every firstborn male shall be designated as holy to the Lord"), and they offered a sacrifice according to what is stated in the law of the Lord, "a pair of turtledoves or two young pigeons." (22–24)

Now there was a man in Jerusalem whose name was Simeon; this man was righteous and devout, looking forward to the consolation of Israel, and the Holy Spirit rested on him. It had been revealed to him by the Holy Spirit that he would not see death before he had seen the Lord's Messiah. Guided by the Spirit, Simeon came into the temple, and when the parents brought in the child Jesus, to do for him what was required under the law, Simeon took him in his arms and praised God, saying, "Master, now you are dismissing your servant in peace, according to your word; for my eyes have seen your salvation, which you have prepared in the presence of all peoples, a light for revelation to the Gentiles and for the glory of your people Israel." And the child's father and mother were amazed at what was being said about him. Then Simeon blessed them and said to his mother Mary, "This child is destined for the falling and the rising of many in Israel, and to be a sign that will be opposed so that the inner thoughts of many will be revealed— and a sword will pierce your own soul too." (25–35)

There was also a prophet, Anna the daughter of Phanuel, of the tribe of Asher. She was of a great age, having lived with her husband seven years after their marriage, then as a widow to the age of eighty-four. She never left the temple but worshiped there with fasting and prayer night and day. At that moment she came, and began to praise God and to speak about the child to all who were looking for the redemption of Jerusalem. (36–38)

When they had finished everything required by the law of the Lord, they returned to Galilee, to their own town of Nazareth. The child grew and became strong, filled with wisdom; and the favor of God was upon him. (39–40)

EXPLORING THE GOSPEL

The Naming of Jesus

During the Christmas season, the Catholic liturgy celebrates not only the birth of Jesus but, one week later, on the first day of January, the feast of Mary, the Mother of God. This feast is a relatively new celebration. Until the recent reform of the Church calendar, it was the feast of the Holy Name of Jesus. Though the emphasis has shifted to Mary, the *Theotokos* or God-bearer, its gospel reading is still that of the circumcision and naming of Jesus, which were previously its main focus and are mentioned in Luke 2:21. Circumcision marks Jesus with the external sign of membership in the covenant community, but it is his naming that is allotted greater prominence by Luke, stressing that the name *Jesus* was given him by the angel even before his conception.

AFTER EIGHT DAYS HAD PASSED, IT WAS TIME TO CIRCUMCISE THE CHILD. . . .

... AND HE WAS CALLED JESUS, THE NAME GIVEN BY THE ANGEL BEFORE HE WAS CONCEIVED IN THE WOMB.

To Name and To Call

There is something mysterious in every name. In biblical understanding, a person's name contains the essence of the person—it *is* the person—and the giving of a name bestows an identity that determines a person's calling. The name *Jesus*, or *Iesus*, is a Latinized spelling of the Greek *Iesous* as found in the gospels. What lies behind the Greek form is the Aramaic name *Yeshua*. Aramaic is the language that was familiarly spoken by Jesus, and *Yehsu*, a shortened form, is likely the name by which he was known. Behind this Aramaic name lies the Hebrew form, *Yehoshua*, or *Joshua* in English, whose meaning is "Yahweh saves" or "the Lord will save." This is the new name given by Moses to Hoshea, son of Nun (Nm 13:16), *Hoshea* meaning *salvation*. As Moses' successor, Joshua is the New Moses who leads the People of Israel across the Jordan and into the Promised Land. Jesus (*Yeshua*) is therefore presented in the gospels as the New Moses, the one who comes to save God's people, the one who *is* salvation.

Name and Identity

To change a person's name is to bestow a new identity and a new calling. Jacob is given a new name, *Israel*, in Genesis 32:29, and with it a new vocation for a people yet to be born. Jesus gives Simon a new name, *Peter*, in Matthew 16:18, and a new role in his new community. While Jesus' true identity is mysterious, so too is your own, which is bound up with his. At the core of your being is the Christ-self, bestowed on you in baptism with your name. This is your truest, deepest self, fashioned in his image. In Isaiah 62:2 is the promise to Zion, "You shall be called by a new name that the mouth of the Lord will give," and in the Book of Revelation we find similar words addressed to one of the seven churches: "I will give a white stone, and on the white stone is written a new name that no one knows except the one who receives it." The journey of self-discovery is a journey to the interior, where we meet the one who has known us from the beginning, who calls us by name.

The Presentation in the Temple

Nonetheless, for the circumcision and naming of Jesus, Luke gives us only one single verse. It is the presentation of Jesus at the Temple in Jerusalem, however, that really surrounds him with prayer, the prayer of Simeon and Anna, who both praise God for the child. Once again we are reminded of the story of Samuel, who, after he was weaned, was brought to the house of the Lord at Shiloh and given to the Lord (1 Sm 1:24–28).

ENTERING INTO CONTEMPLATION

1. CHOOSE WHERE YOU WILL PRAY
   COMPOSE YOURSELF FOR PRAYER

Find a quiet place where you can be alone and uninterrupted for an hour. Take time to be still, to be present to God, and to express both your longing to know the mind and heart of Jesus and your desire to follow him more faithfully in your daily life.

2. IMAGINE THE SCENE

The setting is the Temple courtyard. Place yourself among those gathered there. See the baby, *Yeshua*, in the arms of Mary. Let the sound of these soft syllables sink into your mind and heart: *Yeshua—the Lord is salvation, the Lord saves, the Lord is saving. . . .* This tiny child *is* salvation. This tiny child is *my* salvation. See Simeon take the child in his arms, and hear him chant his canticle of praise, known still by its Latin opening, *Nunc dimities—Now you are dismissing*. This hymn of praise has become part of the Church's night prayer, recited daily by many as they prepare to close their eyes in sleep. See ancient Anna, who prays in the Temple night and day (2:37), as she joins this little group praying and prophesying.

GUIDED BY THE SPIRIT, SIMEON CAME INTO THE TEMPLE, AND WHEN THE PARENTS BROUGHT IN THE CHILD JESUS, TO DO FOR HIM WHAT WAS REQUIRED UNDER THE LAW, SIMEON TOOK HIM IN HIS ARMS AND PRAISED GOD, SAYING, "MASTER, NOW YOU ARE DISMISSING YOUR SERVANT IN PEACE, ACCORDING TO YOUR WORD; FOR MY EYES HAVE SEEN YOUR SALVATION. . . ."

AT THAT MOMENT SHE CAME, AND BEGAN TO PRAISE GOD AND TO SPEAK ABOUT THE CHILD TO ALL WHO WERE LOOKING FOR THE REDEMPTION OF JERUSALEM.

3. ASK FOR THIS GRACE

Jesus, draw me into the mystery of your name, the mystery of your presentation.

4. LISTEN TO WHAT THE PERSONS SAY

Simeon's words, like his arrival in the Temple, seem prompted by the Holy Spirit (2:25). They are addressed to God as "Master," they look forward to his approaching death, and they speak of salvation for the gentile nations as well as for Israel. They also prophesy division among many and pain for the child's mother. We are given none of Anna's words, but we can imagine spontaneous praise on her lips, like that of Hannah (who is likely Luke's source for her name) in 1 Samuel 2:1–10.

5. ENTER INTO CONVERSATION

How can you speak to Jesus? What can you say to him? Perhaps all you can do is whisper his name, "*Yeshua, Yeshua,* my Savior, my Salvation." His mysterious and sacred name becomes your prayer. There is power in the name of Jesus, but at this moment it seems to speak only of vulnerability. You hear Simeon's prophetic words to Mary, and Anna's words of praise as she brings the good news about the birth of a divine savior to all who are longing for the redemption of *Yerushalayim*—the Holy City Jerusalem—that it might be rid of oppressors and freed from its captors. Speak to Anna or to Simeon if you feel moved to do so, and enter into their praising of God.

6. ENTER INTO SILENCE

As these mysterious elderly figures withdraw again into their own prayer, enter with them into their silence. Or go quietly with Mary and Joseph and the child Jesus as they return to Nazareth to begin their simple village life together as a family, one family hidden, as it were, among many others, but with a treasure in their arms and much to ponder in their hearts.

7. CONCLUSION

Thank Jesus for all that you have experienced in this prayer.

AFTER PRAYING

1. REFLECT ON THE EXPERIENCE

At the end of your contemplation, move to another place and spend a few minutes reviewing your experience of prayer, making note of those things that brought you either consolation or desolation, so that, if you do a repetition or application of the senses, you can return to them again, and enter more deeply into the mystery you are contemplating.

2. QUESTIONS THAT MAY ARISE OUT OF PRAYER

As you contemplate these scenes, is there a sense that the Second Person of the Trinity has freely chosen to take on all the helplessness and vulnerability of an infant, and come into this world out of love and compassion for you in particular? Do you feel your heart moved with love and compassion for him in his poverty?

3. SEARCHING THE SCRIPTURES

You may want to turn to the Psalms and prayerfully read words that might have been on the lips of any pious Jewish person going up to the Temple of the Lord, for instance Psalm 24, which speaks of ascending the hill of the Lord and standing in the holy place (verse 3), or Psalm 72, dedicated to Solomon, the son of David, that he may defend the poor and deliver the needy (verse 4).

What to Pray on Next

If you have completed two contemplations, make a repetition and then an application of senses, ending the day in a more passive prayer and allowing yourself to be drawn deeper into appreciation and gratitude. If you have done only one contemplation, go on the final passage (D). Try not to be anxious about what you did not choose to pray on or about what graces you may have missed. Allow the Holy Spirit to guide you, just as the Spirit guided the persons you are contemplating.

Before You Pray

1. Read the gospel passage slowly and carefully, seeking to understand it more deeply in its totality or in its parts as you wish.

2. Read the section Exploring the Gospel as an aid both to understanding the text and to stimulating your imagination when you pray.

3. Before you begin to pray, read the passage once again.

D. GROWING IN PRAYER: THE MYSTERY OF HIS CALLING

LUKE 2:41—52

Now every year his parents went to Jerusalem for the festival of the Passover. And when he was twelve years old, they went up as usual for the festival. When the festival was ended and they started to return, the boy Jesus stayed behind in Jerusalem, but his parents did not know it. Assuming that he was in the group of travelers, they went a day's journey. Then they started to look for him among their relatives and friends. When they did not find him, they returned to Jerusalem to search for him. After three days, they found him in the Temple, sitting among the teachers, listening to them and asking them questions. And all who heard him were amazed at his understanding and his answers. When his parents saw him they were astonished, and his mother said to him, "Child, why have you treated us like this? Look, your father and I have been searching for you in great anxiety." He said to them, "Why were you searching for me? Did you not know that I must be in my Father's house?" But they did not understand what he said to them. Then he went down with them and came to Nazareth, and was obedient to them. His mother treasured all these things in her heart. (41–51)

And Jesus increased in wisdom and in years, and in divine and human favor. (52)

EXPLORING THE GOSPEL

A Vocation Narrative

The finding of the boy Jesus in the Temple presents us with another parallel to the First Book of Samuel: the vocation narrative in 1 Samuel 3. The tradition of the rabbis held that Samuel was twelve years of age at this time, and so Luke describes Jesus as being twelve years old (2:42). Though there is no restatement of Jesus' name, which marks the account of Samuel's calling by God as a true-to-form vocation narrative ("Samuel! Samuel!"), Luke seems nonetheless to make clear that Jesus also has a special calling: "I must be in my Father's [house]" (2:49). This seems to be the preferred translation, "house" being understood, thus implying that Jesus must be in the Temple (that is, the house of the Lord), just as Samuel had to remain in the shrine or temple at Shiloh.

Our Personal Vocation

Each of us has a special calling, not only a calling to *do* something but a calling to *be* someone special. Jesus is called eventually to teach and to heal, but here he says simply, "I must be . . ." Few of us can spend our lives in the Temple, like Simeon and Anna, but each of is called to *be* a temple—to live in the awareness of an inner sacred space where God dwells.

The Adolescent Jesus

Though Jesus receives his calling in his naming, he still has to grow to maturity before he can fully appropriate his calling and understand it. He already has a deep awareness of God as his Father: this is a relationship that transcends every other. When his family makes their annual pilgrimage to the Holy City, he is drawn to the house of God, the Temple in Jerusalem. Luke presents us with a believable adolescent, idealistic and wholly absorbed in what he feels is his vocation. As an adolescent, Jesus has yet to learn that such whole-hearted devotion to his heavenly Father can actually cause pain to his parents.

HE SAID TO THEM, "WHY WERE YOU SEARCHING FOR ME? DID YOU NOT KNOW THAT I MUST BE IN MY FATHER'S HOUSE?"

AFTER THREE DAYS, THEY FOUND HIM IN THE TEMPLE, SITTING AMONG THE TEACHERS, LISTENING TO THEM AND ASKING THEM QUES-TIONS.

ENTERING INTO CONTEMPLATION

1. CHOOSE WHERE YOU WILL PRAY
COMPOSE YOURSELF FOR PRAYER

Find a quiet place where you can be alone and uninterrupted for an hour. Take time to be still, to be present to God, and to express both your longing to know the mind and heart of Jesus and your desire to follow him more faithfully in your daily life.

2. IMAGINE THE SCENE

Make yourself present in some way, perhaps as a child of the same age as Jesus, or as a friend of his parents, who accompanies them in the search for their lost son. Once again, try to imagine the Temple courtyard, with its various areas defined by rows of pillars. If Jesus was there for three days, much of his time would have been spent in prayer—private prayer, as well as the kind of public prayer in which Zechariah took part earlier (1:8–10). This is where Jesus will later spend much of his Judean ministry teaching. Try to see him now as a young boy, already deeply engaged in learning, sitting among the teachers, almost as an equal, listening and asking questions. See the astonishment in the eyes of Mary and Joseph when, after three days, they finally discover him. No doubt they would have rushed to Jesus to embrace him as soon as they saw him.

3. ASK FOR THIS GRACE

Jesus, draw me into the mystery of your calling.

4. LISTEN TO WHAT THE PERSONS SAY

What thoughts go through a parent's mind when a child goes missing? Hear the anguish in Mary's voice as she questions Jesus. Listen to his innocent, ingenuous response.

5. ENTER INTO CONVERSATION

What do you say to reassure his parents? Perhaps it is with Jesus that you are most drawn to talk. What is this sense of vocation, of special calling, that he has become aware of? How has it emerged over time? Share with him your own sense of calling, or ask him to help you become more aware of it.

6. ENTER INTO SILENCE

His parents do not understand Jesus' actions. They do not understand his answers.

Perhaps it's with hearts full of conflicting emotions that they depart together—Mary and Joseph grateful to have found Jesus safe and sound, but puzzled at his behavior and his strange response, while Jesus, glad to have had this experience of freedom to explore where his inner promptings may be leading him, is also regretful at having caused so much consternation to his parents. Go with them and enter into their silent reflections.

7. CONCLUSION

Thank Jesus for all that you have experienced in this prayer.

AFTER PRAYING

1. REFLECT ON THE EXPERIENCE

At the end of your contemplation, move to another place and spend a few minutes reviewing your experience of prayer, making note of those things that brought you either consolation or desolation, so that, if you do a repetition or application of the senses, you can return to them again, and enter more deeply into the mystery you are contemplating.

BUT THEY DID NOT UNDERSTAND WHAT HE SAID TO THEM.

What to Pray on Next

Having contemplated two of the passages in this chapter, repeat them together in order to deepen your experience of being drawn into Jesus' prayer. Jesus will continue to grow in wisdom and understanding. It will be almost twenty years before he begins his teaching. These were not years spent impatiently marking time until he could embark on his mission. He must have entered as fully as possible into the ordinary daily life of the family and the village. In the application of senses, imagine the simplicity and goodness of this kind of life, even in the midst of difficulties and hardships.

2. QUESTIONS THAT MAY ARISE OUT OF PRAYER

In contemplating the boyhood of Jesus, and especially the "hidden life" of his ensuing years in Nazareth, do you grow in understanding of why Jesus would actually want to spend so many years in a tiny village in the northern part of Israel, an area that was neglected and even despised by many? (Matthew 4:15, quoting Isaiah 9:1, refers to it as a land of Gentiles, a place of darkness.) Do you feel that Jesus wants to enter into the ordinariness of *every* person's life, of *your* life?

3. SEARCHING THE SCRIPTURES

The gospel writers expect that their readers will know the First (or Old) Testament well enough to catch their many allusions to its books. Since Luke is building his infancy narrative largely on material in the First Book of Samuel, it would be good to go back and read chapter 3 of this ancient text, to see how Luke makes use of the account of the boy Samuel and his calling to serve the Lord as a prophet to all Israel (1 Sm 4:1).

II.

JESUS' PRAYER AND THE HOLY SPIRIT

Read the preparatory material below and choose two of the following passages for today's prayer.

A. *Preparing the Way with Prayer:*

   The Mystery of His Mission

   Luke 3:1–18

B. *Anointed in Prayer:*

   The Mystery of His Baptism

   Luke 3:21–22

C. *Tested in Prayer:*

   The Mystery of His Heart

   Luke 4:1–13

D. *Preaching in Prayer:*

   The Mystery of His Word

   Luke 4:14–30

There is a dynamic element in every gospel, but especially in that of Luke, and that is the power of the Holy Spirit.

BACKGROUND

The Holy Spirit in the Gospel of Luke

The Holy Spirit is mentioned more often in the Gospel of Luke than in any other gospel—at least seven or eight times in the first two chapters alone. We are told that John will be filled with the Holy Spirit even before his birth (1:15), and that Jesus will be conceived when the Holy Spirit comes upon Mary (1:35). We see Elizabeth filled with the Holy Spirit when the child leaps in her womb at the sound of Mary's voice (1:41), and we see Zechariah filled with the Holy Spirit at the circumcision and naming of John (1:67). Later we find the Holy Spirit mentioned three times in connection with Simeon and the presentation of Jesus in the Temple (2:25, 26, 27). In these ways, the Holy Spirit is shown as surrounding the mysterious origins of both John and Jesus, but Luke makes clear that Jesus, unlike John, is actually conceived through "the power of the Most High" (that is, through the Holy Spirit), and that he will be holy and will be called Son of God (1:35).

Jesus and the Holy Spirit

When we come to chapter 3 and the beginning of Jesus' public ministry, Luke again introduces the Holy Spirit, first in John's proclamation that the Messiah will baptize with the Holy Spirit and with fire (3:16), and then in the descent of the Holy Spirit on Jesus after his baptism (3:22). After this, Jesus, full of the Holy Spirit, is led by the Spirit into the wilderness (4:1). Then, filled with the Holy Spirit (4:14), he returns to Nazareth, where he proclaims from the scroll of Isaiah, "The Spirit of the Lord is upon me . . ." (4:18).

Jesus' Unique Possession of the Holy Spirit

If Jesus' prayer—his own inner communing with God—has a unique quality, it must be because of his special relationship to the Father in and through the Holy Spirit. Prayer runs like a golden thread through the Gospel of Luke, but the presence and power of the Holy Spirit is also there, especially at important moments in the first half of this gospel. Jesus possesses the Holy Spirit in a unique way, and it is in the Spirit that his prayer has its life. But the prayer of Jesus is about more than simply his own secret relationship with God in the Spirit. Prayer is, surely, the secret of his personal attraction. It is his hidden inner life, which draws others to him. But Jesus did not cultivate this communion with the Father for its own sake or for his own sake. He has a mission, and his prayer, like that of all the great prophets before him, is the prayer of intercession for those to whom and for whom he is sent.

Jesus Empowered by the Spirit

It is in his baptism that Jesus receives his mission from the Father and is empowered by the Spirit to undertake it, beginning in his hometown of Nazareth. This baptism is preceded by John's preaching in the desert, while Jesus' preaching in Nazareth is prepared for by his prayer and fasting in that same Judean wilderness. Behind Luke's account of the appearance on the scene of John and Jesus lies the history of Israel's great prophetic figures, Moses and Elijah, in whose mission the desert had significance as a place of testing and conversion, of refuge and revelation. Jesus, the new Joshua, will also be the new Moses inaugurating a New Covenant, and John, "with the spirit and power of Elijah" (Lk 1:17), will prepare the way for Jesus.

A. Preparing the Way with Prayer: The Mystery of His Mission

Luke 3:1–18

Before You Pray

1. Read the gospel passage slowly and carefully, seeking to understand it more deeply in its totality or in its parts as you wish.

2. Read the section Exploring the Gospel as an aid both to understanding the text and to stimulating your imagination when you pray.

3. Before you begin to pray, read the passage once again.

In the fifteenth year of the reign of the Emperor Tiberius, when Pontius Pilate was governor of Judea, and Herod was ruler of Galilee, and his brother Philip ruler of the region of Ituraea and Trachonitis, and Lysanias ruler of Abilene, during the high priesthood of Annas and Caiaphas. The Word of God came to John son of Zechariah in the wilderness. He went into all the region around the Jordan, proclaiming a baptism of repentance for the forgiveness of sins, as it is written in the book of the words of the prophet Isaiah, "The voice of one crying out in the wilderness: 'Prepare the way of the Lord, make his paths straight. Every valley shall be filled, and every mountain and hill shall be made low, and the crooked shall be made straight, and the rough ways be made smooth, and all flesh shall see the salvation of God.'" (3:1–6)

John said to the crowds that came out to be baptized by him, "You brood of vipers! Who warned you to flee from the wrath to come? Bear fruits worthy of repentance. Do not begin to say to yourselves, 'We have Abraham as our ancestor'; for I tell you, God is able from these stones to raise up children to Abraham. Even now the ax is lying at the root of the tree; every tree, therefore that does not bear good fruit is cut down and thrown into the fire." (7–9)

And the crowds asked him, "What then should we do?" In reply he said to them, "Whoever has two coats must share with anyone who has none; and whoever has food must do likewise."

Even tax collectors came out to be baptized, and they asked him, "Teacher, what should we do?" He said to them, "Collect no more than the amount prescribed for you." Soldiers also asked him, "What should we do?" He said to them, "Do not extort money from anyone by threats or false accusations, and be satisfied with your wages." (10–14)

As the people were filled with expectation, and all were questioning in their hearts concerning John, whether he might be the Messiah, John answered all of them by saying, "I baptize you with water; but one who is more powerful than I is coming; I am not worthy to untie the thong of his sandals. He will baptize you with the Holy Spirit and fire. His winnowing fork is in his hand, to clear his threshing floor and to gather the wheat into his granary; but the chaff he will burn with unquenchable fire." (15–17)

So, with many other exhortations, he proclaimed the good news to the people. (18)

EXPLORING THE GOSPEL

The Prayer of John the Baptist

The desert is the desolate abode of evil spirits—a place of trial and testing. It is also the privileged place of prayer, where the word of the Lord came to Elijah in the cave at Horeb and then in the sound of sheer silence or, as the *Revised Standard Version* puts it, "a still small voice" (1 Kgs 19:12). What was said of Jeremiah—"This is a man who loves the family of Israel and prays much for the people and the holy city" (2 Mc 15:14)—could be said of all the prophets, including John the Baptist. While his prayer is not mentioned, except to say that he taught his disciples to pray (Lk 11:1), we can imagine that John's days and nights in the wilderness, perhaps even from his youth (Lk 1:80), must have been spent largely in prayer. John had to prepare the way for the Messiah with preaching and with the purification of a people, but the primary purification was surely his own, through fasting (Luke, unlike Mark and Matthew, doesn't tell us

H E WENT INTO ALL THE REGION AROUND THE JORDAN, PROCLAIMING A BAPTISM OF REPENTENCE FOR THE FORGIVENESS OF SINS. . . .

what John ate), and the primary preparation was also his own, through prayer, attuning himself to the still small voice of the Spirit, and opening himself to receive the word of God.

A New Beginning

The opening of Luke's third chapter echoes the opening of the book of the Prophet Haggai, announcing the coming of the word of God to the prophet, naming the ruler and specifying the year of his reign in which this word was given (Hg 1:1). It, thus, formally marks a real beginning—a beginning of the gospel proper.

The Herald of Good Tidings

The quotation from Isaiah (40:3–5), which is meant to show John as the fulfillment of this prophetic passage, comes from what is called *The Book of the Consolation of Israel* (Is 40-55), whose opening words are: "Comfort, O comfort my people, says your God. Speak tenderly to Jerusalem" (40:1). The prophet is told to "Cry out!" (40:6) He is to be the "herald of *good tidings*" (40:9)—that is, of good news or gospel. He is to say to the cities of Judah, "Here is your God!" (40:9), who "comes with might" (40:10), but who will also be compassionate: "He will feed his flock like a shepherd; he will gather the lambs in his arms" (40:11). We can imagine John being familiar with this passage, resonating with it in his prayer, wondering what the Messiah will be like, and wondering what his own role will be.

Called to Conversion

Just as Israel is called by John to repentance, so each of us is called to ever deeper levels of conversion—conversion of mind and heart and will, to be carried out through decision and action. Though we cannot change our nature or who we are, we can change our ways of thinking and choosing, we can change our attitudes and our affectivity—our ways of loving especially. We can even choose whether we will be joyful or miserable, grateful or resentful in dealing with the situations that life sends us. A time of retreat—a day or even an hour of prayer—is a

... AS IT IS WRITTEN IN THE BOOK OF THE WORDS OF THE PROPHET ISAIAH, "THE VOICE OF ONE CRYING OUT IN THE WILDERNESS: 'PREPARE THE WAY OF THE LORD, MAKE HIS PATHS STRAIGHT. EVERY VALLEY SHALL BE FILLED, AND EVERY MOUNTAIN AND HILL SHALL BE MADE LOW, AND THE CROOKED SHALL BE MADE STAIGHT, AND THE ROUGH WAYS BE MADE SMOOTH, AND ALL FLESH SHALL SEE THE SALVATION OF GOD.'"

time of withdrawal from external distractions into an interior landscape, a sacred space, where we meet our deepest, truest self. It is there also that we can freely open our self to the presence of the Spirit who dwells within.

ENTERING INTO CONTEMPLATION

JOHN SAID TO THE CROWDS THAT CAME OUT TO BE BAPTIZED BY HIM, "YOU BROOD OF VIPERS! WHO WARNED YOU TO FLEE FROM THE WRATH TO COME? BEAR FRUITS WORTHY OF REPENTANCE."

1. CHOOSE WHERE YOU WILL PRAY
    COMPOSE YOURSELF FOR PRAYER

Find a quiet place where you can be alone and uninterrupted for an hour. Take time to be still, to be present to God, and to express both your longing to know the mind and heart of Jesus and your desire to follow him more faithfully in your daily life.

2. IMAGINE THE SCENE

We are told that crowds came out to be baptized by John (Lk 3:7). John is calling the whole of Israel to conversion, to prepare a people fit to receive the Messiah when he appears. He goes "into all the region around the Jordan" (3:3), and people of all walks of life come to him there.

3. ASK FOR THIS GRACE

Jesus, draw me into the mystery of your prophetic mission.

4. LISTEN TO WHAT THE PERSONS SAY

In Luke's account, John calls the crowd a brood of vipers (3:7), though in Matthew's gospel these words are addressed to the Pharisees and Sadducees. Ordinary people and tax collectors and even Herod's Jewish soldiers all ask in turn, "What should we do?" John is gentler in his response to them, yet very direct and concrete. Perhaps some stayed on for a while to talk with him, to seek out his wisdom as they tried to understand the scriptures and his proclamation of repentance. You might try to see yourself as one of these seekers of wisdom. Since Ignatian contemplation is aimed at conversion and directed toward action, your prayer can also make use of this same question, "What then should *I* do?"

5. ENTER INTO CONVERSATION

As you go into the wilderness to converse with John, you can ask how you might prepare yourself in prayer to listen to the Spirit, to recognize Jesus more easily and more readily receive him in your daily life, so that you can follow him more faithfully. When the crowds disperse and you find yourself alone with John, what do you say to him? What does he say to you?

6. ENTER INTO SILENCE

Let Jesus' words touch your heart and his presence move you. Enter into attentive, affective silence with him.

7. CONCLUSION

Thank Jesus for all that you have experienced in this prayer.

AFTER PRAYING

1. REFLECT ON THE EXPERIENCE

At the end of your contemplation, move to another place and spend a few minutes reviewing your experience of prayer, making note of those things that brought you either consolation or desolation, so that, if you do a repetition or application of the senses, you can return to them again, and enter more deeply into the mystery you are contemplating.

"I BAPTIZE YOU WITH WATER; BUT ONE WHO IS MORE POWERFUL THAN I IS COMING; I AM NOT WORTHY TO UNTIE THE THONG OF HIS SANDALS. HE WILL BAPTIZE YOU WITH THE HOLY SPIRIT AND FIRE."

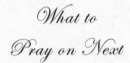

What to Pray on Next

You may feel moved to follow this contemplation with another on John the Baptist. The prophetic calling to proclaim the word of God often brings opposition, persecution, suffering, and even death to the prophet. John's arrest and imprisonment (Lk 3:19–20) and his eventual martyrdom foreshadow what lies in store for the prophet Jesus. Or you may wish to turn to one of the passages that follow.

2. QUESTIONS THAT MAY ARISE OUT OF PRAYER

Since John is calling the people of Israel to conversion, you might ask yourself what this call stirs up in you. What is the area of conversion that you are being called to deepen? Where do you need to be freed or healed? To what degree of generosity is the Holy Spirit inviting you? How are the subtle workings of the Spirit different from those of the counter-spirits you sense within you?

3. SEARCHING THE SCRIPTURES

The verses from the beginning of *The Book of the Consolation of Israel* (Is 40–55), are the backdrop of Luke's account of John the Baptist's ministry. A prayerful reading of Isaiah 40:1–11 could follow your contemplation.

B. ANOINTED IN PRAYER: THE MYSTERY OF HIS BAPTISM

LUKE 3:21–22

Before You Pray

1. Read the gospel passage slowly and carefully, seeking to understand it more deeply in its totality or in its parts as you wish.

2. Read the section Exploring the Gospel as an aid both to understanding the text and to stimulating your imagination when you pray.

3. Before you begin to pray, read the passage once again.

Now when all the people were baptized, and when Jesus also had been baptized and was praying, the heaven was opened, and the Holy Spirit descended upon him in bodily form like a dove. And a voice came from heaven, "You are my Son, the Beloved; with you I am well pleased. (21–22)

EXPLORING THE GOSPEL

The End of John's Ministry

It is worth noting that, from Luke's account, it would seem that John the Baptist is imprisoned even *before* Jesus is baptized (3:19–20), and we are not told who actually baptizes him (3:21) or whether he immerses himself. Perhaps this is Luke's way of showing that John's ministry is now ended while that of Jesus is about to begin.

The Beginning of Jesus' Mission

Because he has already made clear, in the infancy narrative, who Jesus is—that he will be called the Son of the Most High (1:32), and that he is a Savior, the Messiah, the Lord (2:11)—Luke

AND A VOICE CAME FROM HEAVEN, "YOU ARE MY SON, THE BELOVED; WITH YOU I AM WELL PLEASED."

does not describe Jesus' baptism. He simply mentions it as having occurred when all the people had been baptized. Baptism is what brings Jesus into solidarity with "all the people"—with all those for whom he has come and to whom he is missioned.

Jesus' Anointing with the Spirit

Luke's focus here is not on Jesus' baptism but on the descent of the Holy Spirit on Jesus, and, at this important moment, he presents Jesus, after having been baptized, as praying. Later, in his second volume, the Acts of the Apostles, Luke will reflect on this descent of the Spirit as a messianic *anointing*: "God anointed Jesus of Nazareth with the Holy Spirit and with power" (Acts 10:38). In the light of Luke's later understanding, we can say that it is this gift of the Spirit that reveals more fully to Jesus his mission as the Messiah, the Christ, the Anointed One, even if this wording is not found in the text of Luke's gospel.

The Source of Jesus' Authority

Who, besides Jesus himself, is aware of this anointing with the Spirit? If we look only at the words spoken by the heavenly voice ("You are my Son, the Beloved; with you I am well pleased" [Lk 3:22]), it would seem that they are addressed to Jesus alone, and that he alone hears them. Luke, however, has the Holy Spirit descend upon Jesus "in bodily form like a dove" (3:22), which might indicate that this anointing is seen by others who are present. This may explain why Jesus will later refer to John's baptism when questioned about his authority (Lk 20:1–8), implying that this gift of the Spirit—which many saw descend at his baptism—is the witness of his authority. In any case, the words spoken from heaven reaffirm for Jesus himself what was told to Mary in the annunciation: "He will be called Son of God" (Lk 1:35). God is the source of his authority.

ENTERING INTO CONTEMPLATION

1. CHOOSE WHERE YOU WILL PRAY
COMPOSE YOURSELF FOR PRAYER

Find a quiet place where you can be alone and uninterrupted for an hour. Take time to be still, to be present to God, and to express both your longing to know the mind·and heart of Jesus and your desire to follow him more faithfully in your daily life.

2. IMAGINE THE SCENE

In this scene we see Jesus, at some moment between his baptism and his anointing with the Spirit, poised in prayer. This is the first time that Luke presents Jesus as praying, and it signals the importance of what is about to take place. Is Jesus aware that he is about to be seized by the Spirit—the Spirit that will enable him to appropriate and accept his mission as Messiah? We cannot know. We can only try to imagine what went on within him. In the *Spiritual Exercises*, Ignatius Loyola has us ask for interior knowledge of Jesus—for knowledge of his mind and heart. Even though his interiority is beyond us, we know that Jesus had, besides a divine consciousness, a human consciousness, an interior life not totally unlike our own. Like us, he had to trust in the Father, and so, like us, he prayed.

3. ASK FOR THIS GRACE

Jesus, draw me into the mystery of your baptism and anointing.

4. LISTEN TO WHAT THE PERSONS SAY

You may wish to place yourself in this scene as someone who has been baptized by John with Jesus and is drawn to this mysterious figure in prayer. How do you picture him? Is he standing and speaking aloud in the traditional Jewish posture of prayer, or is he seated and praying silently? You may not want to intrude in this sacred communion, but you can try to imagine what

. . . WHEN JESUS ALSO HAD BEEN BAPTIZED AND WAS PRAYING, THE HEAVEN WAS OPENED. . . .

... THE HOLY SPIRIT
DESCENDED UPON HIM
IN BODILY FORM LIKE A
DOVE.

passes between him and the Father. While Jesus' baptism ritualizes his oneness with the whole people of Israel, we can be sure that his desire goes beyond his own people. It is a desire to be one with all of humanity—with each one of us.

5. ENTER INTO CONVERSATION

You might ask in prayer to have a deeper desire to be one with Jesus, to "put on" (Eph 4:24) more and more completely his mind and heart, his way of seeing and his way of loving. Imagining yourself as baptized with Jesus may bring to mind your own Christian baptism into Jesus' death and resurrection and your own anointing with the Holy Spirit. You too are poised in prayer, expectant. Allow yourself to be drawn into conversation with Jesus. Share with him how you have lived out your baptism—your readiness to go into the tomb with him in all the many opportunities that have presented themselves in your life. Talk with Jesus about all that is stirring in your heart.

6. ENTER INTO SILENCE

Just be there with Jesus in his silent communion in the Spirit.

7. CONCLUSION

Thank Jesus for all that you have experienced in this prayer.

AFTER PRAYING

1. REFLECT ON THE EXPERIENCE

At the end of your contemplation, move to another place and spend a few minutes reviewing your experience of prayer, making note of those things that brought you either consolation or desolation, so that, if you do a repetition or application of the senses, you can return to them again, and enter more deeply into the mystery you are contemplating.

2. QUESTIONS THAT MAY ARISE OUT OF PRAYER

How do you desire *now* to live out your baptismal covenant in the future? What feelings are stirred up in you? Are you aware of the Spirit of Jesus drawing you into deeper union with him and moving you to commit yourself to him anew? Do you experience any anxiety about the demands of following Jesus—about the cost of discipleship?

3. SEARCHING THE SCRIPTURES

Jesus' baptism in the waters of the Jordan and the descent of the Spirit upon him may call to mind the words of Ezekiel in chapter 36:24–28, which are often read at the baptism of infants: "I will sprinkle clean water upon you . . . I will put my spirit within you." Again this is something that you could read and reflect on after your contemplation.

What to Pray on Next

If you are spending the whole day on retreat and have already contemplated two gospel passages, it would be good to go back to what touched you or to what seemed to hold more grace for you, and try to enter more deeply into that experience. If you have contemplated only one gospel passage, then go on to one of those that follow.

Before You Pray

1. Read the gospel passage slowly and carefully, seeking to understand it more deeply in its totality or in its parts as you wish.

2. Read the section Exploring the Gospel as an aid both to understanding the text and to stimulating your imagination when you pray.

3. Before you begin to pray, read the passage once again.

C. TESTED IN PRAYER: THE MYSTERY OF HIS HEART

LUKE 4:1–13

Jesus, full of the Holy Spirit, returned from the Jordan and was led by the Spirit in the wilderness, where for forty days he was tempted by the devil. He ate nothing at all during those days, and when they were over, he was famished. The devil said to him, "If you are the Son of God, command this stone to become a loaf of bread." Jesus answered him, "It is written, 'One does not live by bread alone.'" (4:1–4)

Then the devil led him up and showed him in an instant all the kingdoms of the world. And the devil said to him, "To you I will give their glory and all this authority; for it has been given over to me, and I give it to anyone I please. If you, then, will worship me, it will all be yours." Jesus answered him, "It is written, 'Worship the Lord your God, and serve only him.'" (5–8)

Then the devil took him to Jerusalem, and placed him on the pinnacle of the temple, saying to him, "If you are the Son of God, throw yourself down from here, for it is written, 'He will command his angels concerning you, to protect you,' and 'On their hands they will bear you up, so that you will not dash your foot against a stone.'" Jesus answered him, "It is said, 'Do not put the Lord your God to the test.'" When the devil had finished every test, he departed from him until an opportune time. (9–13)

EXPLORING THE GOSPEL

Beginning in the Desert

Once again we are in the desert, the traditional setting for fasting and prayer. Since this is also the dwelling place of evil spirits, this is where Jesus will be confronted by the devil, the one Ignatius Loyola calls simply "the enemy" (*Spiritual Exercises*, paragraph 314, etc). The stage is being set for Jesus' public ministry. He is described as being full of the Holy Spirit, who leads him into the desert—not a desert of sandy wastes but the barren, mountainous Judean wilderness. Since Jesus will later go off frequently to deserted places to pray, especially before important moments in his ministry, it is fitting that he should spend a prolonged period of prayer in this desert before beginning his mission.

Tempted in the Desert

The Greek word for *temptation* also means *testing* or *proving*. In this sense, the desert continues to be a proving ground, a place where, in our own day, motorized vehicles and military equipment are tested under extreme conditions of heat and cold and aridity. Human beings also continue to trek across barren desert wastes, testing their own limits of endurance. So in Luke's gospel Jesus is tested by the devil to see whether he will renounce his human nature and prove that he is the divine Son of God, just as he will be tested later in his ministry: "This generation is an evil generation; it asks for a sign . . ." (Lk 11:29). He will finally be tested at his Crucifixion: "If you are the King of the Jews, save yourself!" (Lk 23:37), and "Are you not the Messiah? Save yourself and us!" (Lk 22:39). Thus, if we go beyond testing to temptation, we can readily see that Jesus may well have been tempted during the course of his ministry to use divine power to overcome the opposition that he so frequently encountered. The scenes in the desert serve to dramatize and prefigure very real temptations that will come later.

... FOR FORTY DAYS HE WAS TEMPTED BY THE DEVIL.

JESUS, FULL OF THE HOLY SPIRIT, RETURNED FROM THE JORDAN AND WAS LED BY THE SPIRIT IN THE WILDERNESS. . . .

Alone in the Desert

There were no eyewitnesses to his encounters with the evil spirit, but even if other people had been with him, what would they have seen? The real temptations would have been internal. How do they come to be recorded as part of the tradition about Jesus? It is possible that he may have spoken to his disciples about his experiences, since twice in this gospel he talks to them about encounters with Satan: "I watched Satan fall from heaven like lightning" (Lk 10:18), and "Simon, Simon, listen! Satan has demanded to sift you like wheat, but I have prayed for you . . ." (Lk 22:31).

The Exodus in the Desert

These scenes also allude to Israel's testing in the wilderness of Sinai. Jesus defeats the devil with the word of God, and the passages he quotes are all from the Book of Deuteronomy, recalling the Exodus experience. The first quotation (Dt 8:3) is worth citing more fully, since it gives the context that elucidates the gospel scenes:

> Remember the long way that the Lord your God has led you these forty years in the wilderness, in order to humble you, testing you to know what was in your heart, whether or not you would keep his commandments. He humbled you by letting you hunger, then by feeding you with manna, with which neither you nor your ancestors were acquainted, in order to make you understand that one does not live by bread alone, but by every word that comes from the mouth of the Lord. (8:2–3)

Like Israel, Jesus is tested in order to reveal what is in his heart. In times of retreat, we too are led into the wilderness to reveal what is in our heart.

ENTERING INTO CONTEMPLATION

1. CHOOSE WHERE YOU WILL PRAY
    COMPOSE YOURSELF FOR PRAYER

Find a quiet place where you can be alone and uninterrupted for an hour. Take time to be still, to be present to God, and to express both your longing to know the mind and heart of Jesus and your desire to follow him more faithfully in your daily life.

2. IMAGINE THE SCENE

Though Jesus is unaccompanied in the desert, imaginative contemplation allows us great freedom. If you can imagine Jesus in the Judean wilderness, you can also take the liberty to imagine yourself in the wilderness with him. Perhaps you are there because you are a passing pilgrim, or a traveler on a journey. Or you can simply be there as yourself: you want to be with Jesus, wherever he happens to be.

3. ASK FOR THIS GRACE

Jesus, draw me into the mystery of your heart.

4. LISTEN TO WHAT THE PERSONS SAY

"If you are the son of God . . ." In the scenes that Luke gives us, he shows the devil twice challenging Jesus to prove that he is the Son of God, challenging the very relationship between Father and Son that was affirmed by the voice from heaven at the descent of the Holy Spirit after his baptism. Jesus' identity, divine and human, would seem to be central to his experience of prayer and fasting in the desert. His prayer, arising out of a heart full of the Holy Spirit and out of a mind filled with the word of God, must have deepened and strengthened his sense of identity as the divine Son of God. His fasting, while it confirmed that he lived not on bread alone but most of all on God's word, would also have put him in touch with his frail and vulnerable human nature. It is this humanity that Jesus is being asked to deny, as though it were only a pretense.

THE DEVIL SAID TO HIM, "IF YOU ARE THE SON OF GOD, COMMAND THIS STONE TO BECOME A LOAF OF BREAD."

HE ATE NOTHING AT ALL DURING THOSE DAYS, AND WHEN THEY WERE OVER, HE WAS FAMISHED.

5. ENTER INTO CONVERSATION

If you are drawn into conversation with Jesus as you contemplate him in his praying and fasting, you may be led to speak to him about his sense of identity and his experience of being human. Did he struggle with the temptation to use any power other than love to achieve his mission? What would you like to ask Jesus? What does he say to you?

6. ENTER INTO SILENCE

After listening to Jesus and being moved by his words, let the immense silence of the desert wilderness enfold you both.

7. CONCLUSION

Thank Jesus for all that you have experienced in this prayer.

AFTER PRAYING

1. REFLECT ON THE EXPERIENCE

At the end of your contemplation, move to another place and spend a few minutes reviewing your experience of prayer, making note of those things that brought you either consolation or desolation, so that, if you do a repetition or application of the senses, you can return to them again, and enter more deeply into the mystery you are contemplating.

2. QUESTIONS THAT MAY ARISE OUT OF PRAYER

Perhaps you will find yourself speaking to Jesus of your own sense of identity, of your own temptations, and of your own experience of what it is to be human—to be spirit and flesh, to be conscious of both strength and fragility. You may be moved to worship Jesus. Are you also able to talk to this extraordinary person—this Son of God, this son of man (Dn 7:13)—as one human being to another?

3. SEARCHING THE SCRIPTURES

You have already read the passage from Deuteronomy 8:2–3, cited earlier. It is worth re-reading in relation to the experiences of spiritual desolation that sometimes come upon us, which God permits in order to humble us and test us (Rules for the Discernment of Spirits, *Spiritual Exercises*, paragraph 322).

What to Pray on Next

If you have done two gospel contemplations and a repetition to deepen your experience, then end the day with a quiet prayer of presence for an hour, gratefully soaking in all the graces received. If you have only completed one contemplation, go on to the final passage, follow it with a repetition on both passages, and end with the prayer of presence. The aim is not to use all the material offered, but to allow the Spirit to guide your choices.

Before You Pray

1. Read the gospel passage slowly and carefully, seeking to understand it more deeply in its totality or in its parts as you wish.

2. Read the section Exploring the Gospel as an aid both to understanding the text and to stimulating your imagination when you pray.

3. Before you begin to pray, read the passage once again.

D. PREACHING IN PRAYER: THE MYSTERY OF HIS WORD

LUKE 4:14-30

Then Jesus, filled with the power of the Spirit, returned to Galilee, and a report about him spread through all the surrounding country. He began to teach in their synagogues and was praised by everyone. (14–15)

When he came to Nazareth, where he had been brought up, he went to the synagogue on the sabbath day, as was his custom. He stood up to read, and the scroll of the prophet Isaiah was given to him. He unrolled the scroll and found the place where it was written: "The Spirit of the Lord is upon me, because he has anointed me to bring good news to the poor. He has sent me to proclaim release to the captives and recovery of sight to the blind, to let the oppressed go free, to proclaim the year of the Lord's favor." And he rolled up the scroll, gave it back to the attendant, and sat down. The eyes of all in the synagogue were fixed on him. Then he began to say to them, "Today this scripture has been fulfilled in your hearing." All spoke well of him, and were amazed at the gracious words that came from his mouth. They said, "Is not this Joseph's son?" He said to them, "Doubtless you will quote to me the proverb, 'Doctor, cure yourself!' And you will say, 'Do here also in your hometown the things that we have heard you did at Capernaum.'" And he said, "Truly I tell you, no prophet is accepted in the prophet's hometown. But the truth is, there were many widows in Israel in the time of Elijah, when the heaven was shut up three years and six months, and there was a severe famine over all the land; yet Elijah was sent to none of them except to a widow at Zarephath in Sidon. There were also many lepers in Israel in the time of the prophet Elisha, and none of them was cleansed except Naaman the Syrian." When they heard this, all in the synagogue were filled with rage. They got up, drove him out of the town, and led him to the brow of the hill on which their town was built, so that they might hurl him off the cliff. But he passed through the midst of them and went on his way. (16–30)

EXPLORING THE GOSPEL

Jesus Returns to Nazareth

Jesus now leaves Judea and returns to the more familiar northern territory of Galilee. He is literally "in the power of the Spirit," as the Greek text puts it—still filled with the Holy Spirit that descended on him after his baptism in the Jordan. He goes about teaching in the region's synagogues, and favorable reports about him begin to circulate. Luke does not describe these prior activities, but chooses instead to begin his account of Jesus' ministry with His return to Nazareth, the town where he grew up and lived for thirty years (Lk 3:23). His rejection by his own townspeople picks up Simeon's prophecy that Jesus is destined to be "a sign that will be opposed" (Lk 2:34), and at the same time it foreshadows his ultimate rejection.

Jesus Goes to the Synagogue

Luke's gospel is the only one to stress that it was Jesus' practice to go to synagogue every Sabbath—not only to take part in worship but also to teach (Lk 4:15). It was probably the custom in the synagogue to read from the prophetic books after the reading of the Torah. Jesus goes up to the pulpit or lectern to read and is given the scroll of the prophet Isaiah. He unrolls it, consciously choosing the passage he wants from Second Isaiah (which begins at Isaiah 61:1), whose opening words recall the events after his baptism: "The Spirit of the Lord is upon me, because he

THEN JESUS, FILLED WTH THE POWER OF THE SPIRIT, RETURNED TO GALILEE, AND A REPORT ABOUT HIM SPREAD THROUGH ALL THE SURROUNDING COUNTRY.

has anointed me. . . ." In saying that these words are fulfilled in the hearing of those present (Lk 4:21), Jesus seems to imply that his anointing is as a prophet rather than as Messiah, since he clearly refers to himself as a prophet when he then says that no prophet is accepted in his hometown (Lk 4:24).

Jesus Announces His Mission

He is anointed as prophet to proclaim good news (literally "to gospel" or "to evangelize"). What this means is spelled out in the rest of the passage: his mission is to bring a word of hope to the poor, to captive slaves or those in prison (for instance, for debt), to the blind, to the oppressed—and not only a word of hope but also fulfillment of this word through deeds of power. The liberation that Second Isaiah announced to exiles in Babylon, Jesus now presents as his own program. It is fulfilled even as it is being heard. The time of deliverance has begun, now is the year of the Lord's favor.

The Context of Synagogue Prayer

As you begin to contemplate this dramatic moment in Jesus' mission, the synagogue setting reveals its context: public prayer on the Sabbath. It is an ideal setting for Jesus, both because it is one of prayer based on the reading of God's word (the Torah and the prophets), and because custom allowed for the invitation of visitors to read and to comment on the scriptures. Jesus would have entered into the profession of faith with which the synagogue service begins: "Hear, O Israel! The Lord is our God, the Lord alone" (Dt 6:4). He would have joined in the prayers. He would have listened attentively to the traditional reading from part of the Pentateuch—the five Books of Moses—and, still filled with the power of the Spirit, he would gladly have accepted the invitation to read from the scroll of Isaiah, and then comment on it.

"THE SPIRIT OF THE LORD IS UPON ME, BECAUSE HE HAS ANOINTED ME TO BRING GOOD NEWS TO THE POOR."

When Jesus sits down to teach (the traditional posture), the eyes of everyone in the synagogue are fixed on him (4:20). His townspeople are impressed with his eloquence, but their praise soon turns to questioning: "Isn't this Joseph's son?" (4:22). Isn't he one of us? How can he then pretend to teach us!

ENTERING INTO CONTEMPLATION

1. CHOOSE WHERE YOU WILL PRAY
   COMPOSE YOURSELF FOR PRAYER

Find a quiet place where you can be alone and uninterrupted for an hour. Take time to be still, to be present to God, and to express both your longing to know the mind and heart of Jesus and your desire to follow him more faithfully in your daily life.

2. IMAGINE THE SCENE

If you situate yourself among the congregation, you do not have to place yourself with those who reject Jesus. You could be there as someone (perhaps a youngster) who is filled with admiration for Jesus. As you feel what it is like to be part of a village community, you may begin to appreciate how this solidarity can make it difficult if not impossible for anyone to rise above the community's "lowest common denominator."

3. ASK FOR THIS GRACE

Jesus, draw me into the mystery of your Word.

4. LISTEN TO WHAT THE PERSONS SAY

How quickly those who think they know Jesus can turn against him. "Isn't this Joseph's son?" (4:22). Isn't he one of us? How can he then pretend to teach us? Then there are Jesus'

HE SAID TO THEM, "DOUBTLESS YOU WILL QUOTE TO ME THE PROVERB, 'DOCTOR, CURE YOURSELF!'"

words about the prophets Elijah and Elisha, to whom he compares himself. You can see why the villagers find these words offensive.

5. ENTER INTO CONVERSATION

If almost the whole village is present in the synagogue, then no doubt his mother Mary is there, as well as many of his extended family (usually referred to as his "brothers"—see Luke 8:19–21). Are you drawn to speak with any one of these? Luke seems to imply that something about Jesus allows him to slip through the crowd—something majestic but not miraculous, or it would mean giving in to their demand for a sign. Perhaps he simply stands in his own truth and stares everyone down. You find yourself drawn to follow him. When you are alone together, say what is in your heart.

6. ENTER INTO SILENCE

Enter with Jesus into his sadness and into that truth of who he is, which is beyond words.

7. CONCLUSION

Thank Jesus for all that you have experienced in this prayer.

AFTER PRAYING

1. REFLECT ON THE EXPERIENCE

At the end of your contemplation, move to another place and spend a few minutes reviewing your experience of prayer, making note of those things that brought you either consolation or desolation, so that, if you do a repetition or application of the senses, you can return to them again, and enter more deeply into the mystery you are contemplating.

"Truly I tell you, no prophet is accepted in the prophet's hometown."

2. QUESTIONS THAT MAY ARISE OUT OF PRAYER

Jesus says things that challenge the assumptions of his fellow townsman. Does what he says also challenge any of your own assumptions—for instance, about what preaching should be, or about how God should work? Jesus is not cowed by the hostility and violence of those around him. What do you think he does to escape from them? Sometimes it is enough to stand in one's own truth to make others back down. What is it about Jesus that is so attractive to you?

3. SEARCHING THE SCRIPTURES

Jesus, driven out of Nazareth, will eventually be cast out of Jerusalem. You may want to read over the passage in which Jeremiah is rejected for prophesying the destruction of Jerusalem, and thrown into an empty, muddy cistern before finally being rescued (Jer 38:1–13).

What to Pray on Next

After two gospel contemplations and a repetition, end the day with an application of the senses, tasting and savoring all that you have received in this day, and move into a quiet prayer of presence. Then glance at the next chapter to see what you might feel moved to pray on tomorrow.

III.

JESUS' PRAYER WITH HIS DISCIPLES

Read the preparatory material below and choose two of the following passages for today's prayer.

A. *Choosing in Prayer:*

   The Mystery of His Wisdom

   Luke 6:12–16

B. *Confessed in Prayer:*

   The Mystery of His Identity

   Luke 9:18–27

C. *Transfigured in Prayer:*

   The Mystery of His Divinity

   Luke 9:28–36

D. *Ecstatic in Prayer:*

   The Mystery of His Joy

   Luke 10:17–24

"Put out into the deep . . ." (Lk 5:4). The call to follow Jesus is an invitation to deeper and deeper levels of conversion.

BACKGROUND

Jesus Calls His Disciples

At Capernaum in Galilee, Jesus attracts his first disciples. Luke's account of their call is somewhat different from that of Matthew and Mark. The account begins with Jesus teaching and healing in the synagogue on the Sabbath: "with authority and power he commands the unclean spirits, and out they come! And a report about him began to reach every place in the region" (4:36–37). Jesus leaves the synagogue and goes to Simon's house, where he heals Simon's mother-in-law of a fever (4:38–39). This is his first encounter with Simon. Crowds gather at sundown and continue to come for healing, which seems to go on all through the night. To escape the crowds, Jesus goes at daybreak to a lonely place (4:42), his preferred setting for prayer (5:16). They seek him out and even try to prevent him from leaving, but Jesus tells them that he was sent to proclaim the good news of the kingdom of God to the other cities also, and goes on his way (4:42–44).

The Disciples Leave Everything

The narrative continues with the miraculous catch of fish (5:1–11), which appears to occur some time later, and which is not found in Matthew or Mark, though it is similar to the post-resurrection appearance in John 21:1–11. It begins on the shore of Lake Gennesaret—the Sea of Galilee—where Jesus, to avoid the crowd pressing in on him, gets into Simon's boat and sits down to teach. Then he asks Simon to move out into deep water and lower his nets. Having toiled all through the night and caught nothing, Simon reluctantly agrees, and unexpectedly fills his nets and the boat with fish, so that he has to call on his partners James and John for help in order to avoid sinking. Simon is overwhelmed, and so are his partners. Bringing their boats to shore, they leave everything and follow Jesus.

Simon Peter's Special Role

Simon is not directly "called" by Jesus. He follows him as the result not only of this extraordinary display of his power but also because of the promise made explicitly to him: "Do not be afraid; from now on you will be catching people" (5:10). This elaborate narrative, with its focus on Simon, signals the special role that he will have as the first of Jesus' disciples. It also demonstrates from the start the esteem that Luke has for him and the special treatment he will receive in this gospel.

Jesus Chooses the Twelve

Levi the tax-collector is called soon afterward by Jesus: "Follow me," and he also abandons everything and follows him (5:27–28). Many more disciples begin to gather around

Jesus. There is something unusual about them. Unlike the disciples of John the Baptist and those of the Pharisees, Jesus' disciples do not fast, probably because Jesus himself no longer fasts (5:33). Neither are they very strict in their observance of the Sabbath: they pluck and eat heads of grain on their way through the fields (6:1), in violation of the law against such "work," at least as the Pharisees interpret it. Jesus will instruct and teach the disciples, but this formation will be as much by his example as by his words. It is during these earlier days that Jesus chooses a select group of disciples to be his close companions. But before naming them, he goes to a mountain to pray, and spends the whole night in prayer to God (6:12).

Becoming Like the Master

If Luke so frequently presents Jesus praying, it is to show that his disciples (including those who read this gospel) must take on his habit of prayer and make it their own. In doing so, they will be drawn into Jesus' relationship with his Father. As they absorb his teachings, they will also observe them in action when they see how Jesus deals with the sick and with sinners, with the outcast and with the poor. Like all good disciples everywhere, they will want to become like their master. For Luke, Jesus' continual communing with God is an essential aspect of who he is, and so it must also be at the center of each disciple's life.

A. CHOOSING IN PRAYER: THE MYSTERY OF HIS WISDOM

LUKE 6:12–16

Before You Pray

1. Read the gospel passage slowly and carefully, seeking to understand it more deeply in its totality or in its parts as you wish.

2. Read the section Exploring the Gospel as an aid both to understanding the text and to stimulating your imagination when you pray.

3. Before you begin to pray, read the passage once again.

Now during those days he went out to the mountain to pray; and he spent the night in prayer to God. And when day came, he called his disciples and chose twelve of them, whom he also named apostles: Simon, whom he named Peter, and his brother Andrew, and James, and John, and Philip, and Bartholomew, and Matthew, and Thomas, and James, son of Alphaeus, and Simon, who was called the Zealot, and Judas, the son of James, and Judas Iscariot, who became a traitor. (6:12–16)

EXPLORING THE GOSPEL

Jesus Spends a Whole Night in Prayer

While Luke frequently shows Jesus praying before some significant event, he has Jesus spend an *entire night* in prayer before choosing the Twelve. This would seem to indicate a very momentous event indeed! His prayer takes place on a mountain. Mountains are closer to heaven, that is,

... H E SPENT THE

NIGHT IN PRAYER TO

GOD.

to the throne of God, which is why shrines and temples are built on mountain tops, and so this setting also bestows significance, as does the mention of God. God is involved in the choice that Jesus is about to make. If Jesus is fully human as well as divine, if he has to grow in wisdom (Lk 2:52), then we can imagine him calling on God's help for the discernment he is engaged in and for the decisions that will follow. It would be a mistake to think that Jesus foresaw during his prayer all that was to ensue later (for instance, the betrayal by Judas Iscariot), or that God was simply dictating a list of those whose names were already divinely determined. Yet he has some knowledge of his disciples that leads him to choose as he does, and he must have hopes and desires for each of them.

A Contemplation Best Made in the Middle of the Night

That Jesus prays through the night is in keeping with ancient traditions of prayer mentioned repeatedly in the scriptures and especially in the Psalms: "on his law they meditate day and night" (Ps 1:2), and "I bless the Lord who gives me counsel; in the night also my heart instructs me" (Ps 16:7), and "I think of you on my bed, and meditate on you in the watches of the night" (Ps 63:6). The practice of keeping vigil, or watching through the night, is enshrined in Holy Saturday's Easter Vigil, which originally ended with the celebration of the Eucharist at the rising of the sun on Easter Sunday morning. In the *Spiritual Exercises*, Ignatius encourages an hour of prayer at midnight or in the middle of the night. It may be helpful, therefore, to make this contemplation after midnight in order to experience something of what Jesus experienced—the solitude and the stillness that only nighttime can bring, or a glimpse of the vastness of the starry sky, which Ignatius loved to gaze at.

ENTERING INTO CONTEMPLATION

1. CHOOSE WHERE YOU WILL PRAY
    COMPOSE YOURSELF FOR PRAYER

Find a quiet place where you can be alone and uninterrupted for an hour. Take time to be still, to be present to God, and to express both your longing to know the mind and heart of Jesus and your desire to follow him more faithfully in your daily life.

2. IMAGINE THE SCENE

The Twelve are those who will not only be Jesus' companions on his journeys, but also his Apostles—those he will send out later on mission. This implies that disciples are called in order to be sent. The list of the names of the Twelve differs slightly in the first three gospels, but Simon, who Jesus re-named Peter, is always first, and with him are always Andrew, his brother, and James and John. The order of some of the other names may change in the gospels, and even the names themselves may vary: it is possible that the one Luke calls "Judas the son of James" is identical with the person called "Thaddaeus" in Matthew and Mark (perhaps, like Simon Peter, he was known by two names). Without presuming to place yourself among the Twelve, you can nonetheless imagine Jesus, praying about *you* and calling you personally by name. Like the shepherd who knows each of his sheep individually, the risen Jesus now knows each and every one of his disciples intimately, and he desires to be known and loved by each of us.

3. ASK FOR THIS GRACE

Jesus, draw me into the mystery of your wisdom.

AND WHEN DAY CAME, HE CALLED HIS DISCIPLES AND CHOSE TWELVE OF THEM. . . .

WHAT IS MY SPE-
CIAL MISSION?

4. LISTEN TO WHAT THE PERSONS SAY

Luke does not presume to tell us how Jesus prayed. But, as you yourself enter into prayer in the middle of the night, you may begin to experience something of what he experienced—the stillness, the solitude, the sense of being alone in the vastness of the darkened night. If you are able to glimpse the sky, able to see the moon or the stars, you can remind yourself: this is the same sky that Jesus gazed upon. Without too much effort, you might imagine that Jesus would likely have recalled the words of Psalm 8:

> When I look at the heavens, the work of your fingers,
>
> the moon and the stars that you have established;
>
> What are human beings that you are mindful of them,
>
> mortals that you care for them? (Ps 8:3–4)

The word *mortals* here translates *ben Adam*, the *Son of Man*, the only title that Jesus used to refer to himself. In his prayer, Jesus would have known that, while God is mindful of every human being, the Father was also especially mindful of Jesus, the Son in whom he is well pleased. In a similar way, Jesus is mindful of all his disciples, and of each in particular. Jesus is mindful at this moment of you.

5. ENTER INTO CONVERSATION

Does Jesus have a word for you? Do you have a word to say to him? You may well have experienced being called earlier by Jesus to follow him in some way, but he continues to call and invite you to go deeper in your relationship with him. You might ask him, "What *is* my personal calling? How am I called *now* to witness to my special relationship with you? What is my special mission? To what or to whom am I being sent?"

6. ENTER INTO SILENCE

In the stillness of the night let your heart also become still, and your mind quieted. Let your heart speak to Jesus' heart and his heart speak to yours. Let your will become one with his. As heart speaks to heart, words become unnecessary.

7. CONCLUSION

Thank Jesus for all that you have received in this prayer.

AFTER PRAYING

1. REFLECT ON THE EXPERIENCE

At the end of your contemplation, move to another place and spend a few minutes reviewing your experience of prayer, making note of those things that brought you either consolation or desolation, so that, if you do a repetition or application of the senses, you can return to them again, and enter more deeply into the mystery you are contemplating.

2. QUESTIONS THAT MAY ARISE OUT OF PRAYER

If you can imagine Jesus choosing and calling you, he must have some purpose in mind. What *are* his hopes for you? What are the longings of his heart? God has planted desires in your heart: what are your own longings, your own deepest desires? How can these become one with Jesus' desires for you?

3. SEARCHING THE SCRIPTURES

The story of Moses' vocation and mission in the Book of Exodus (3:1–12) is worth reading in the light of the calling and missioning of the disciples of Jesus. The doubling of Moses' name ("Moses, Moses!"), when God calls to him from the middle of the burning bush, marks this as a

WHEN THE LORD SAW THAT HE HAD GONE OVER TO LOOK, GOD CALLED TO HIM FROM WITHIN THE BUSH, "MOSES! MOSES!" AND MOSES SAID, "HERE I AM" (EX 3:4).

What to Pray on Next

If this is your first contemplation, prayed in the middle of the night, choose a second passage for your prayer in the morning, from one of the next sections—B, C, or D.

true-to-form vocation narrative. Moses' calling is the result of God's response to the plight of the people of Israel, whose misery in Egypt God has seen and whose cry God has heard (3:7). The calling, as always, is for the sake of sending: "So come, I will send you to Pharaoh to bring my people, the Israelites, out of Egypt" (3:10).

B. CONFESSED IN PRAYER: THE MYSTERY OF HIS IDENTITY

LUKE 9:18–27

Once when Jesus was praying alone, with only the disciples near him, he asked them, "Who do the crowds say that I am?" They answered, "John the Baptist; but others, Elijah; and still others, that one of the ancient prophets has arisen." He said to them, "But who do you say that I am?" Peter answered, "The Messiah of God." (9:18–20)

He sternly ordered and commanded them not to tell anyone, saying, "The Son of Man must undergo great suffering, and be rejected by the elders, chief priests, and scribes, and be killed, and on the third day be raised." (21–22)

Then he said to them all, "If any want to become my followers, let them deny themselves and take up their cross daily and follow me. For those who want to save their life will lose it, and those who lose their life for my sake will save it. What does it profit them if they gain the whole world, but lose or forfeit themselves? Those who are ashamed of me and of my words, of them the Son of Man will be ashamed when he comes in his glory and the glory of the Father and of the holy angels. But truly I tell you there are some standing here who will not taste death before they see the kingdom of God." (23–27)

Before You Pray

1. Read the gospel passage slowly and carefully, seeking to understand it more deeply in its totality or in its parts as you wish.

2. Read the section Exploring the Gospel as an aid both to understanding the text and to stimulating your imagination when you pray.

3. Before you begin to pray, read the passage once again.

H E SAID TO THEM, "BUT WHO DO YOU SAY THAT I AM?"

EXPLORING THE GOSPEL

Jesus Asks a Question

Once again, the scene begins with Jesus' praying—this time "alone, with only the disciples near him" (9:18)—signaling that what is about to follow is significant. Peter's confession of faith in Jesus as "the Messiah of God"—the anointed one—is a turning point in this gospel: a moment of recognition. Called forth by the question to the disciples—"But who do you say that I am?"—Peter's answer is implicitly affirmed by Jesus himself, who immediately orders them not to tell anyone. The reply comes not only to the question of what the disciples think Jesus' true identity is and of what the crowds think, but also as an answer to Herod's question, posed earlier in this same chapter: ". . . who is this about whom I hear such things?" (9:9). Herod Antipas, the Tetrarch or Ruler of Galilee, son of Herod the Great—King of Judea at the time of Jesus' birth (1:5)—would see any claimant to the title of Messiah as a threat to his own position and a challenge to his masters, the Romans. The command of silence only heightens the sense of danger surrounding Jesus.

Jesus Predicts His Passion

The danger is real and even imminent, and it leads Jesus to make the first prediction of his suffering and death at the hands of the elders, chief priests, and scribes, who comprise the governing body of the Great Sanhedrin in Jerusalem. It is toward Jerusalem that Jesus will soon set out (9:51). This prediction includes also the announcement that he will be raised on the third day. What Luke does *not* mention is the rebuking of Jesus by Peter, or Jesus' harsh response to him. Though Luke makes use of much other material from Mark's gospel, with his reverence for Peter he often omits things that would cast the leader of the Apostles in an unfavorable light. Jesus' prayer at the beginning of this scene would suggest that his life and his death are in the hands of his Father, and, while he may not foresee everything in detail, it is clear enough that, like John the Baptist and like the prophets before him, he is heading for a confrontation with the political-religious powers.

Jesus Defines Discipleship

Here, then, we have a fuller answer to the question of who Jesus is: he is not only the Messiah of God but will also be a suffering Messiah, whose death will be the most shameful imaginable, and whose triumph over death will be beyond imagining. We also have an answer to the question of discipleship: discipleship means self-denial, the daily taking up of one's own cross, and the following of Jesus in suffering and death.

Jesus Addresses You

The question that Jesus puts to the Twelve is the question he puts to all his disciples: "Who do you say that I am?" It is not a matter of what others are saying today, or even of what contemporary scholars may say. Jesus asks each one of us, "What do *you* say? Who am I for *you*?" Your answer will have to take into account that knowing and loving Jesus means following him. It will also have to include the cost of discipleship as spelled out by Jesus himself—self-denial and the daily taking up of your own personal cross and a faithful following in the path that he walks.

The Call of Jesus

Jesus' words find an echo in the contemplation on "The Call of the King" in the *Spiritual Exercises*, where Ignatius has Christ the Eternal King say, "It is My will to conquer all the world and all enemies and so enter into the glory of My Father; therefore, whoever would like to come with Me is to labor with Me, that following Me in the pain, he may also follow Me in the glory" (paragraph 95). This call is addressed to all and yet to each person in particular. The stress is not on suffering but on Jesus himself and on *being with him*, who desires so much to be with us, no matter what the cost to him.

"IF ANY WANT TO BECOME MY FOLLOWERS, LET THEM DENY THEMSELVES AND TAKE UP THEIR CROSS DAILY AND FOLLOW ME. FOR THOSE WHO WANT TO SAVE THEIR LIFE WILL LOSE IT, AND THOSE WHO LOSE THEIR LIFE FOR MY SAKE WILL SAVE IT."

"BUT TRULY I TELL YOU THERE ARE SOME STANDING HERE WHO WILL NOT TASTE DEATH BEFORE THEY SEE THE KINGDOM OF GOD."

ENTERING INTO CONTEMPLATION

1. CHOOSE A PLACE TO PRAY
COMPOSE YOURSELF FOR PRAYER

Find a quiet place where you can be alone and uninterrupted for an hour. Take time to be still, to be present to God, and to express both your longing to know the mind and heart of Jesus and your desire to follow him more faithfully in your daily life.

2. IMAGINE THE SCENE

Since Jesus' words about following him are addressed not just to the Twelve but to the other disciples as well—"to them all" (9:23)—you can easily place yourself among them. Allow his gaze to engage yours and to penetrate you with understanding and acceptance and love.

3. ASK FOR THIS GRACE

Jesus, draw me into the mystery of your identity, the mystery of who you are.

4. LISTEN TO WHAT THE PERSONS SAY

As you imagine the exchange between Jesus and his disciples, and as you hear Peter's response, imagine also that Jesus addresses you directly when he asks, "Who do you say that I am?"

5. ENTER INTO CONVERSATION

How do you put your feelings into words? Allow yourself to be drawn into intimate conversation with Jesus. If you have hesitations or doubts or fears, tell them to him. What would you want Jesus to be for you? What is the deepest longing of your heart right now? Ask him to help you express it.

6. ENTER INTO SILENCE

If your desire is just to be with him, a wordless gesture may be more than enough to convey this.

7. CONCLUSION

Thank Jesus for all that you have received in this prayer.

AFTER PRAYING

1. REFLECT ON THE EXPERIENCE

At the end of your contemplation, move to another place and spend a few minutes reviewing your experience of prayer, making note of those things that brought you either consolation or desolation, so that, if you do a repetition or application of the senses, you can return to them again, and enter more deeply into the mystery you are contemplating.

2. QUESTIONS THAT MAY ARISE OUT OF PRAYER

Why does Jesus move so quickly into prophesying his suffering and death? Is he really eager to suffer? Is he teaching his disciples to embrace suffering? Is he trying to prepare the disciples for what he foresees as inevitable? Is he dispelling false notions the disciples may have about the way to glory? What do his words mean for you right now?

3. SEARCHING THE SCRIPTURES

It would be useful to read over the parallel accounts of Peter's profession of faith in the gospels of Matthew (16:13–28) and Mark (8:18–27). In these two accounts, Peter reacts to Jesus' prediction of his Passion by trying to block his way to Jerusalem (Mt 16:22; Mk 8:32), and Jesus responds with the words, "Get behind me, Satan!" Not so in Luke's account: it is too shocking!

PETER ANSWERED, "THE MESSIAH OF GOD."

If you have prayed on both of the earlier passages, move gently into the repetitions and application of senses. Otherwise, go on to one of the passages in C or D.

This omission reveals something of Luke's reverence for Peter as the head of the Apostles, even though Luke also omits Matthew's very significant passage (16:17–19) in which Jesus changes Simon's name to Peter (*Petros* in Greek, derived from *petra*, rock), and gives him the keys to the gates of heaven, and power to exclude and to welcome back into the fold.

C. TRANSFIGURED IN PRAYER: THE MYSTERY OF HIS DIVINITY

LUKE 9:28-36

Now about eight days after these sayings Jesus took with him Peter and John and James, and went up on the mountain to pray. And while he was praying, the appearance of his face changed, and his clothes became dazzling white. Suddenly they saw two men, Moses and Elijah, talking with him. They appeared in glory and were speaking of his departure, which he was about to accomplish at Jerusalem. Now Peter and his companions were weighed down with sleep; but since they had stayed awake, they saw his glory and the two men who stood with him. Just as they were leaving him, Peter said to Jesus, "Master, it is good for us to be here; let us make three dwellings, one for you, one for Moses, and one for Elijah"—not knowing what he said. While he was saying this, a cloud came and overshadowed them; and they were terrified as they entered the cloud. Then from the cloud came a voice that said, "This is my Son, my Chosen; listen to him!" When the voice had spoken, Jesus was found alone. And they kept silent and in those days told no one any of the things they had seen. (28–36)

Before You Pray

1. Read the gospel passage slowly and carefully, seeking to understand it more deeply in its totality or in its parts as you wish.

2. Read the section Exploring the Gospel as an aid both to understanding the text and to stimulating your imagination when you pray.

3. Before you begin to pray, read the passage once again.

SUDDENLY THEY SAW TWO MEN, MOSES AND ELIJAH, TALKING WITH HIM. THEY APPEARED IN GLORY AND WERE SPEAKING OF HIS DEPARTURE, WHICH HE WAS ABOUT TO ACCOMPLISH AT JERUSALEM.

EXPLORING THE GOSPEL

A Mountaintop Experience

The transfiguration of Jesus occurs, Luke tells us, about a week after Peter's confession of faith. In his account, Jesus leads Peter, John, and James up a mountain for a specific purpose: to pray, and it is while Jesus is praying that his appearance is changed. It is almost as though the intensity of his prayer is what brings on the transformation. The actual mountain is not named, but it is called a holy mountain, and, like every high mountain, it brings those who climb it closer to heaven. Here it brings Jesus into such close contact with the Father that his facial appearance is changed and even his clothing becomes blindingly white.

The Law and the Prophets

The disciples suddenly see Moses and Elijah there in glory with Jesus, speaking with him about his departure—in the original Greek, his *Exodos*—his Exodus or his passing over to join these great symbolic figures, a destiny to be fulfilled in Jerusalem. After its fulfillment, Jesus will explain to the disciples on the road to Emmaus all the things about himself in the scriptures, "beginning with Moses and all the prophets" (Lk 24:27). The cloud that envelopes the figures and terrifies Peter and his companions is like the cloud that descends on Mount Sinai: "The glory of the Lord settled on Mount Sinai, and the cloud covered it for six days; on the seventh day he called to Moses out of the cloud. . . . Moses entered the cloud, and went up on the mountain" (Ex 24:16,18). Here, too, on this mountain a voice speaks from the cloud, not just to Jesus (as at his baptism) but also to the disciples, and identifies Jesus for them, saying, "This is my Son, the Chosen," adding, "Listen to him!" (9:35).

Jesus the Suffering Servant

Coming as it does immediately after Peter's confession of faith, at least in the text of the gospel, this experience provides the disciples with yet another answer to the question of Jesus' identity: Jesus is God's Son, he is the Chosen One. This last title echoes the words of Isaiah 42:1, "Here is my servant, whom I uphold, my chosen, in whom my soul delights," with which the first of the Suffering Servant Songs begins. It is to Jesus above all others that the disciples must listen.

The Mystery of Humility

The mystery of Jesus' divinity is infinite, and carries us beyond the loftiest mountaintop. And yet, he desires to share something of this mystery with Peter and his companions. He desires to share it also with us. His desire to be with us in everything involves him in all our suffering. The source of all this desire is the love of the Trinity, which, in giving birth to all of creation, is drawing all of creation into itself through Jesus. We can hardly imagine all this, but instead of trying to stretch our mind and imagination to comprehend it, perhaps we can enter this mystery of Jesus' identity in another way. The presence of Moses in this scene gives us a way in. In the Book of Numbers 12:3, we are told that "Moses was very humble, more so than anyone else on the face of the earth," and yet, as the Lord makes clear to Aaron and Miriam, "With him I speak face to face—clearly, not in riddles; and he beholds the form of the Lord" (Nm 12:8). Jesus, the Son of God, the Chosen, is humbler still, and it is his infinite humility that draws us into the mystery of who he is and into the mystery of his prayer.

ENTERING INTO CONTEMPLATION

1. CHOOSE WHERE YOU WILL PRAY
   COMPOSE YOURSELF FOR PRAYER

Find a quiet place where you can be alone and uninterrupted for an hour. Take time to be still, to be present to God, and to express both your longing to know the mind and heart of Jesus and your desire to follow him more faithfully in your daily life.

THEN FROM THE CLOUD CAME A VOICE THAT SAID, "THIS IS MY SON, MY CHOSEN; LISTEN TO HIM!"

AND WHILE HE WAS PRAYING, THE APPEARANCE OF HIS FACE CHANGED, AND HIS CLOTHES BECAME DAZZLING WHITE.

2. IMAGINE THE SCENE

The drowsiness of the disciples may indicate that this extraordinary experience occurs at night, as does the fact that they come down the mountain only the next day (9:37). If so, what is this glory that envelopes Jesus in the darkness as he speaks with Moses and Elijah? What is this shining that comes from his whole person? The dwellings that Peter suggests they build are reminiscent of the shelters built during the celebration of the Feast of Booths (Dt 16:13), which in Jesus' time had become a joyous seven-day celebration of pilgrims in Jerusalem after the harvest (Ex 23:16). Perhaps Peter is caught up in this celebration and its spirit of joy. He also seems to want to capture the vision and contain the experience on the mountaintop by building these booths for Moses and Elijah (who would hardly need them) and for Jesus, none of which makes much sense, as Luke points out: "not knowing what he said" (9:33).

3. ASK FOR THIS GRACE

Jesus, draw me into the mystery of your divinity.

4. LISTEN TO WHAT THE PERSONS SAY

Though we are not given the exchange between Jesus, Moses, and Elijah, we do know that it concerns Jesus' coming ordeal. Can you imagine what Jesus might say? We do have Peter's words: "It is good for us to be here." Try to savor the goodness of your being there with Jesus. Listen to the words of the voice from heaven: "This is my Son, my Chosen."

5. ENTER INTO CONVERSATION

It may be easier to speak first to Peter or to one of the other disciples. Do you experience some of their sense of awe and wonder, their confusion and fear? When Jesus is there with them after the revelation of his divinity, is there any conversation with his disciples? If so, try to join in. The desire to know Jesus from within (the "internal knowledge" Ignatius speaks of in the *Spiritual Exercises*, paragraph 104) is not the desire to have your own face and form transfigured, but rather the desire to become more and more like him by sharing in his humility. Ignatius shares this very personal understanding of humility in the meditation on the Three Kinds of Humility (*Spiritual Exercises*, paragraphs 165–167), which are really deeper and deeper levels of love—love for God, love for Jesus, and a loving desire to be like Jesus in everything, even in his poverty and in his humiliation. Allow Jesus himself to draw you humbly and gently into this mystery. Speak with him as with a friend.

6. ENTER INTO SILENCE

In the transfiguration we see something also of the transforming power in prayer. We, too, are changed from within by prayer. In your own prayer you are intentionally in touch with the transforming power of God. There is an awesome silence here that draws you in.

7. CONCLUSION

Thank Jesus for all that you have received in this prayer.

AFTER PRAYING

1. REFLECT ON THE EXPERIENCE

At the end of your contemplation, move to another place and spend a few minutes reviewing your experience of prayer, making note of those things that brought you either consolation or desolation, so that, if you do a repetition or application of senses, you can return to them again, and enter more deeply into the mystery you are contemplating.

JUST AS THEY WERE LEAVING HIM, PETER SAID TO JESUS, "MASTER, IT IS GOOD FOR US TO BE HERE; LET US MAKE THREE DWELLINGS, ONE FOR YOU, ONE FOR MOSES, AND ONE FOR ELIJAH"—NOT KNOWING WHAT HE SAID.

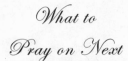

What to Pray on Next

It may be good to read the first chapter of Peter's second letter. It is an exhortation to holiness, and lends itself to meditation on faith, good works, knowledge, self-control, endurance, godliness, mutual affection, and love. The authority for Peter's teaching comes, he says, from having been an eyewitness to Jesus' majesty: he himself heard the voice of God coming from heaven "while we were with him on the holy mountain" (1:18). If you have completed two contemplations, you are ready to go on later to the repetitions and the application of senses. Otherwise pray the passage in the next section, D.

2. QUESTIONS THAT MAY ARISE OUT OF PRAYER

Peter, James, and John are at first terrified by the vision and yet also fascinated by it, so that Peter wants to hold on to it. When you are given gifts of consolation in prayer, do you also try to hold on to them? In clinging to God's gift, do you sometimes forget the giver? Why do you think that St. Ignatius tells us to humble ourselves as much as we can in times of consolation (*Spiritual Exercises*, paragraph 324)?

3. SEARCHING THE SCRIPTURES

The theophany or revelation of God on Mount Sinai is found in chapter 19 of the Book of Exodus. There, God speaks to Moses from a cloud on the mountaintop and, in chapter 20, gives the Law, the Ten Commandments. There is a second giving of the Law in chapter 34. Moses is with the Lord on the mountain, fasting from food and drink for forty days and forty nights (34:28). When at last he comes down, his face is shining so brightly that he is forced to wear a veil (34:29–35).

D. ECSTATIC IN PRAYER: THE MYSTERY OF HIS JOY

LUKE 10:17–24

The seventy returned with joy, saying, "Lord, in your name, even the demons submit to us!" He said to them, "I watched Satan fall from heaven like a flash of lightning. See, I have given you authority to tread on snakes and scorpions, and over all the power of the enemy; and nothing will hurt you. Nevertheless, do not rejoice at this, that the spirits submit to you, but rejoice that your names are written in heaven." (10:17–20)

At that same hour Jesus rejoiced in the Holy Spirit and said, "I thank you, Father, Lord of heaven and earth, because you have hidden these things from the wise and the intelligent and have revealed them to infants; yes, Father, for such was your gracious will. All things have been handed over to me by my Father; and no one knows who the Son is except the Father, or who the Father is except the Son and anyone to whom the Son chooses to reveal him." (21–22)

Then turning to the disciples, Jesus said to them privately, "Blessed are the eyes that see what you see! For I tell you that many prophets and kings desired to see what you see, but did not see it, and to hear what you hear, but did not hear it." (23–24)

SEE, I HAVE GIVEN YOU AUTHORITY TO TREAD ON SNAKES AND SCORPIONS, AND OVER ALL THE POWER OF THE ENEMY; AND NOTHING WILL HURT YOU.

EXPLORING THE GOSPEL

Jesus Welcomes Back His Disciples

On the way to Jerusalem, Jesus is accompanied not only by the Twelve, but by a number of other disciples as well. Of these he appoints seventy or so to go on ahead of him to the various towns and villages that he will visit, to cure the sick and to announce the coming reign of God (10:1–12). When they return, these disciples are filled with joy at the power they exercised in the name of Jesus, and Jesus himself rejoices in the Holy Spirit, praying aloud to God. In the preceding verse (10:16), Jesus says, "Whoever listens to you listens to me . . ." The disciples were sent out to minister in his place, that is, in the person of Jesus, and in the same way that he ministers, relying totally on God for all their needs (10:3–4). Here we see the effects of the power that God exerts through those who speak and heal in Jesus' name: " . . . even the demons submit to us!" (10:17).

Jesus Foresees His Cosmic Struggle

Jesus sees even more: He sees the fall of Satan, which he compares to a flash of lightning from the sky. Even though Satan's power may persist, the disciples' mission reveals that Satan's reign is ended. Jesus alone has authority "over all the power of the enemy" (10:19) (Ignatius' preferred name for Satan), and he now shares this authority with his disciples. Their rejoicing, however, should be centered on their assurance of the joys of heaven rather than on any exercise of power here below—even the power bestowed by Jesus.

Jesus Alone Knows the Father

All this leads up to Jesus' ecstatic praise of God as he rejoices in the Spirit (10:21–24). His prayer here is different from anything we have seen so far. It is as though the joy of the disciples has ignited his own joy, but it is also and primarily a joy in God. It is joy inspired by the Spirit of

God. It is joy in "the Lord of heaven and earth"—whom Jesus addresses directly as *Father*—who reveals hidden things, not to the learned but to his disciples, whom he calls "infants" or little ones (10:21). As for the continuing question of his identity, what Jesus here reveals is that "no one knows who the Son is except the Father" (10:22), and likewise, no one knows "who the Father is except the Son." Jesus alone reveals who the Father is.

Asking to Know the Mind and Heart of Jesus

In asking to be drawn into the mystery of Jesus' joy, you are not asking for ecstatic experiences or special gifts of consolation from God. You are asking only what you have been seeking from the beginning, which is already a great grace: some knowledge of the mind and heart of Jesus, some sense of the joy that he felt in the mission the Father had given him, and in the companions who were part of that mission. The more you come to know, understand, and love Jesus from within, as he really is—in his humanity especially, but also in his whole divine-human self—the more you will love him and be filled with joy and gratitude because of *his* great love for *you*. The mystery you are asking to be drawn into is the mystery of Jesus' whole being, filled with the presence and power of the Holy Spirit that inspires his prayer to the Father, and that energizes every fiber of his body with joy.

ENTERING INTO CONTEMPLATION

1. CHOOSE A PLACE TO PRAY
   COMPOSE YOURSELF FOR PRAYER

Find a quiet place where you can be alone and uninterrupted for an hour. Take time to be still, to be present to God, and to express both your longing to know the mind and heart of Jesus and your desire to follow him more faithfully in your daily life.

"... No one knows who the Son is except the Father, or who the Father is except the Son and anyone to whom the Son chooses to reveal him."

"FOR I TELL YOU THAT MANY PROPHETS AND KINGS DESIRED TO SEE WHAT YOU SEE, BUT DID NOT SEE IT, AND TO HEAR WHAT YOU HEAR, BUT DID NOT HEAR IT."

2. IMAGINE THE SCENE

Jesus' exultation in the Holy Spirit recalls the words that Luke puts on the lips of Mary in the *Magnificat* and that Elizabeth uses of the child in her womb who leaps for joy (1:44, 47). It is exhilaration, wild joy, ecstatic delight. As such, it is a gift of the Holy Spirit—something given only in special moments, and recognized as a gift, as something whose source is other than our self. It need not always be wild and ecstatic. There are times when we are surprised by joy, by a deep and quiet joy rising up like a spring from some secret source within—what Ignatius calls "consolation without a preceding cause" *(Spiritual Exercises*, paragraph 330), by which he means a spiritual consolation given only by God, directly and with no intermediary. Try to imagine how Jesus expresses his joy in his face, his gestures, his body.

3. ASK FOR THIS GRACE

Jesus, draw me into the mystery of your joy.

4. LISTEN TO WHAT THE PERSONS SAY

If you are present in this scene as one of the seventy disciples—one of the little ones—you can try to imagine their joy on returning from their mission. Begin with the joy they express, and with Jesus' words to them. You can also try to sense the great heavenly joy to which Jesus is inviting you, and begin to realize how blessed are the eyes that see what you see, and the ears that hear what you hear, all of which comes to you through the inspired words of this gospel. Then listen to Jesus' own words to the Father.

5. ENTER INTO CONVERSATION

Speak if you can with some of the disciples. Share in their joyful exchange. Speak with Jesus as he shares also in your joy.

6. ENTER INTO SILENCE

After Jesus' ecstatic prayer to the Father, you may be moved by the Spirit to pray aloud also. Or let yourself be drawn into quiet joy—the joy of the Trinity.

7. CONCLUSION

Thank Jesus for all that you have received in this prayer.

AFTER PRAYING

1. REFLECT ON THE EXPERIENCE

At the end of your contemplation, move to another place and spend a few minutes reviewing your experience of prayer, making note of those things that brought you either consolation or desolation, so that, if you do a repetition or application of the senses, you can return to them again, and enter more deeply into the mystery you are contemplating.

2. QUESTIONS THAT MAY ARISE OUT OF PRAYER

What is the role of ecstatic or charismatic prayer in a person's life? Are these gifts that one should ask for in prayer? Are these gifts all of equal importance? We should first of all distinguish the *gift of the Spirit*, given to us in baptism, from the *gifts of the Spirit*, which can take many different forms. There is also something that St. Paul terms, the *fruit of the Spirit*, the effect of the Spirit in our life, as seen in "love, joy, peace, patience, kindness, generosity, faithfulness, gentleness, and self-control. There is no law against such things" (Gal 5:22–23).

3. SEARCHING THE SCRIPTURES

The gifts of the Spirit are still very much alive in the Church today. They seem to have had an even greater prominence in the early Church, confirming the baptism of new Christians with a baptism in the Spirit (Acts 2:38), or being given after baptism by a laying on of hands

THE SEVENTY RETURNED WITH JOY, SAYING, "LORD IN YOUR NAME, EVEN THE DEMONS SUBMIT TO US!"

What to Pray on Next

You have come to the end of the third day. Having made two contemplations, you can then do two repetitions and an application of senses. In between you may find it profitable to read chapter 2, verses 42–47 of the Acts of the Apostles, where Luke gives us a glimpse of the idyllic early days of the Christian community. We get a sense of the peace and joy and prayerful ecstasy that filled the hearts of the first believers to be baptized into Christ, and that made them truly friends in the Lord.

(Acts 7:14–17). These gifts sometimes preceded baptism, showing that God had already given the gift of faith to certain persons, for instance, even to some Gentiles (Acts 10:44–48). In the early Christian communities the gifts of the Spirit, especially the gift of tongues and the gift of prophecy, were sometimes the source of conflict rather than harmony. Paul writes his First Letter to the Corinthians in order to put an end to divisions in the Church at Corinth (1:10–17), and especially to divisions in the celebration of the Lord's Supper (11:17–22). In chapters 12 and 13, Paul gives a teaching on these gifts in all their variety, and establishes a hierarchy among them, from the lowest to the highest (11:27–31), with the gifts of service ranged above the extraordinary gifts (the gift of tongues he puts last). He tells us to "strive for the greater gifts. And I will show you a still more excellent way" (11:31). Then, in chapter 13, he gives his famous peroration on love (*agape* or *caritas*). The highest gifts are the gifts of faith, hope, and love, "and the greatest of these is love" (13:13).

IV.

JESUS' TEACHING ABOUT PRAYER (I)

Read the preparatory material below and choose two of the following passages for today's prayer.

A. *The Lord's Prayer:*

   The Mystery of This Prayer

   Luke 11:1–4

B. *Persistent Prayer:*

   The Mystery of His Shamelessness

   Luke 11:5–8

C. *Effective Prayer:*

   The Mystery of His Trust

   Luke 11:9–13

D. *Carefree Prayer:*

   The Mystery of His Serenity

   Luke 12:22–32

To pray is to enter into a relationship with God. To pray as Jesus prays is to enter into his relationship with God.

BACKGROUND

Jesus' Unique Relationship with God

In ecstatic prayer, Jesus calls God *Father* no less than five times in two verses—twice in direct address (10:21–22). Though Luke does not use the Aramaic word, *Abba*, but only the Greek, *Pater*, we know that *Abba* is implied from its use in Mark's Gospel, 14:36 ("He said, 'Abba, Father, for you all things are possible; remove this cup from me' . . ."), and from its use by Paul in Romans 8:15 ("When we cry, 'Abba! Father!' . . .") and in Galatians 4:6 (". . . God has sent the Spirit of his Son into our hearts, crying, 'Abba! Father!'") This word is unique to Jesus as a way of addressing God, and it expresses something of the unique relationship that Jesus has with God. Seeing Jesus so often at prayer and hearing him pray aloud, the disciples are gradually drawn into his prayer. Eventually one of them asks him to teach them to pray.

Jesus Gives the Disciples a Prayer

Thus, Jesus' teaching about prayer begins with the Lord's Prayer. This is another important moment in Luke's gospel. It should not surprise us, therefore, that he again sets the scene with Jesus praying. The disciples would be familiar with Jewish forms of prayer, and so, in asking Jesus to teach them to pray, they are asking something more: they are asking him to teach them to pray *as he prays*. They make this request, however, in terms of what John the Baptist did for *his* disciples. Perhaps John's disciples had some special prayer that distinguished them from the disciples of the Pharisees. The prayer that Jesus teaches his disciples will mark them and all future disciples as uniquely his. Thus, the Roman Catholic Church has restored a very meaningful ritual in having a copy of the Lord's Prayer given to newly anointed catechumens, together with the creed, in the Rite of Christian Initiation of Adults: it is another significant step in the process of induction into the Community of Disciples, and links them with those to whom Jesus first taught this prayer.

Jesus Invites the Disciples into His Relationship with God

The mystery of Jesus' name, and the power in this name, were touched on above, in chapter I, section C. Here we have yet another powerful and mysterious name. In teaching the Lord's Prayer, Jesus tells the disciples that, when they pray, they are to address God with the same familial, intimate, reverent, yet childlike form that he uses: "*Abba*." In doing so, he is doing much more than revealing the secret name that he uses in prayer. He is, in fact, inviting them into the same intimate, childlike relationship that he has with God—a very great mystery indeed! For this reason the early Church guarded the Lord's Prayer as sacred, and kept it secret from the uninitiated, and reserved the word *Abba* for use in prayer.

Before You Pray

1. Read the gospel passage slowly and carefully, seeking to understand it more deeply in its totality or in its parts as you wish.

2. Read the section Exploring the Gospel as an aid both to understanding the text and to stimulating your imagination when you pray.

3. Before you begin to pray, read the passage once again.

A. THE LORD'S PRAYER: THE MYSTERY OF *THIS* PRAYER

LUKE 11:1–4

Jesus was praying in a certain place, and after he had finished, one of his disciples said to him, "Lord, teach us to pray, as John taught his disciples." He said to them, "When you pray, say: Father, hallowed be your name. Your kingdom come. Give us each day our daily bread. And forgive us our sins, for we ourselves forgive everyone indebted to us. And do not bring us to the time of trial." (11:1–4)

EXPLORING THE GOSPEL

The Father

Luke's version of the Lord's Prayer is somewhat different from the more familiar version in Matthew's gospel (6:9–13). Being shorter—without Matthew's additional words and phrases—it may actually be closer to what Jesus originally taught. It begins, not with "Our Father in heaven," but simply and directly with the word "Father." It does not have the phrase, "Your will be done, on earth as it is in heaven," nor does it conclude with the words, "but rescue us from the evil one." (The translation used here is not the one found in the liturgy of the Mass, but that of the *New Revised Standard Version*, which is used throughout this work.)

The Community

The prayer that Jesus teaches is not an individual prayer but a prayer for the community, since it is given in the plural. After asking that God's name be held holy and that God's kingdom come, the prayer makes three petitions, each of which uses the plural words *us* and *our*. To pray this prayer, then, is to pray in union with all who are already united under the reign of God, pleading that God would extend this reign to the whole world, and that everyone everywhere would acknowledge his holiness. Even when the Lord's Prayer is used to conclude one's private meditation or contemplation, as it is in the *Spiritual Exercises*, it serves to remind us that the kingdom is central to the gospel message, and that extending God's reign is central to our following of Jesus.

The Petitions

The three final petitions bring us before God as children before a dear and loving father, asking for what we need: to be fed, to be forgiven, and to be protected.

ENTERING INTO CONTEMPLATION

1. CHOOSE WHERE YOU WILL PRAY
   COMPOSE YOURSELF FOR PRAYER

Find a quiet place where you can be alone and uninterrupted for an hour. Take time to be still, to be present to God, and to express both your longing to know the mind and heart of Jesus and your desire to follow him more faithfully in your daily life.

2. IMAGINE THE SCENE

You could begin by imagining the place where Jesus is praying, seeing yourself among the disciples, so that, when Jesus finishes praying, it is you who approaches him and asks, "Teach us to pray." If you wish, you could use the method Ignatius suggests at the end of the *Exercises* (The

JESUS WAS PRAYING IN A CERTAIN PLACE, AND AFTER HE HAD FINISHED, ONE OF HIS DISCIPLES SAID TO HIM, "LORD, TEACH US TO PRAY, AS JOHN TAUGHT HIS DISCIPLES."

"FATHER, HALLOWED BE YOUR NAME. YOUR KINGDOM COME. GIVE US EACH DAY OUR DAILY BREAD. AND FORGIVE US OUR SINS, FOR WE OURSELVES FORGIVE EVERYONE INDEBTED TO US. AND DO NOT BRING US TO THE TIME OF TRIAL."

Second Method of Prayer, paragraphs 249–257), praying on one word of the Lukan text at a time, or spending even the entire hour on a single word, if you find relish and consolation in it (paragraph 254). The word *Abba*, with all its associations of childhood longing, would certainly lend itself to this kind of prolonged meditation, and could bring much healing to a heart wounded by the actions or absence of an earthly father. Other words—for instance, the word *kingdom* (or *reign*, whose connotations are more dynamic and suggestive of *becoming*, rather than fixed and static)—might also lend themselves to this kind of meditation, or the phrase *"our daily bread,"* which can include both our daily need for sustenance and our need for the bread that is broken in Eucharist.

3. ASK FOR THIS GRACE

Jesus, draw me into the mystery of this prayer.

4. LISTEN TO WHAT THE PERSONS SAY

As Jesus teaches you this very special prayer, try to hear the words as though for the very first time. Listen to the quality of his voice and to the reverence with which he speaks these words.

5. ENTER INTO CONVERSATION

Here, instead of conversing with Jesus, you could begin by reading the prayer slowly several times before settling on whichever word or phrase draws you in. You are there in the person of Jesus himself, whose words are on your lips. You are in the heart of his prayer. You are in his very heart. You are praying through him. And with him. And in him. He is praying through you; and with you and in you. You are in communion with the Father and with Jesus in the Spirit.

6. ENTER INTO SILENCE

After allowing yourself to be led through the words of the prayer, enter as peacefully as you can into silent communion in the Triune God.

7. CONCLUSION

Thank Jesus for all that you have received in prayer.

AFTER PRAYING

1. REFLECT ON THE EXPERIENCE

At the end of your contemplation or meditation, move to another place and spend a few minutes reviewing your experience of prayer, making note of those things that brought you either consolation or desolation, so that, if you do a repetition or application of the senses, you can return to them again, and enter more deeply into the mystery you are contemplating.

2. QUESTIONS THAT MAY ARISE OUT OF PRAYER

How are you affected by praying the Lord's Prayer? What happens when you enter into this ongoing, ceaseless exchange of love between the Father and the Son? Do you experience a difference in praying Luke's? Which one makes you feel closer to Jesus, Luke's or Matthew's? Which one makes you feel closer to the community of the Church? To the Communion of Saints?

3. SEARCHING THE SCRIPTURES

In the fifth book of Moses, Deuteronomy 6:4, we find the words that are to be recited by Jewish men every morning on rising and every evening before going to sleep: "Hear, O Israel: the LORD is our God, the LORD alone." This creed would therefore have been on the lips of Jesus twice a day, and addressed to Yahweh (whose sacred name was never uttered but always replaced by *ADONAI* or LORD). Jesus, in giving his disciples a prayer, however, addresses God directly as *Abba*, an Aramaic word, showing that Jesus gave this prayer in the vernacular language spoken every day, rather than in Hebrew, the liturgical language used in the synagogue.

What to Pray on Next

Having prayed Luke's version of the Lord's Prayer, you may then want to pray Matthew's (6:9–13). Matthew's is part of the collection of teachings known as the Sermon on the Mount. Luke's is given during Jesus' journey to Jerusalem. We might suspect that Luke's version, simply because it is shorter, is the more original, but there may well be parts of Matthew's version that are closer to what Jesus actually said. Matthew's is certainly the more familiar, and is used by Christians throughout the world.

Before You Pray

1. Read the gospel passage slowly and carefully, seeking to understand it more deeply in its totality or in its parts as you wish.

2. Read the section Exploring the Gospel as an aid both to understanding the text and to stimulating your imagination when you pray.

3. Before you begin to pray, read the passage once again.

B. PERSISTENT PRAYER: THE MYSTERY OF HIS SHAMELESSNESS

LUKE 11:5–8

And he said to them, "Suppose one of you has a friend, and you go to him at midnight and say to him, 'Friend, lend me three loaves of bread; for a friend of mine has arrived, and I have nothing to set before him.' And he answers from within, 'Do not bother me; the door has already been locked, and my children are with me in bed; I cannot get up and give you anything.' I tell you, even though he will not get up and give him anything because he is his friend, at least because of his persistence he will get up and give him whatever he needs." (5–8)

EXPLORING THE GOSPELS

Jesus Gives a Parable

Immediately after giving the disciples the Lord's Prayer, Jesus offers them by way of exhortation a parable that is not found in any of the other gospels. It is about a neighbor's middle-of-the-night request for bread, which may be why it occurs after the prayer that asks for daily bread, though what it really stresses is a way of asking rather than what is asked for. The parable assumes a typically tiny one-room house in which a family is sleeping together on mats on the stone or earthen floor. For the householder to get up in the dark and unbar the door and deal with this request would be to disturb the entire family. And yet he will get up: not to do so would be a shameful violation of the sacred duty of hospitality.

Jesus Teaches Humility

Though Jesus does not make any immediate and explicit application of the parable to prayer, this kind of application is clearly implied at the end of the teaching that follows (11:9–13). What the parable shows is that persistence in prayer will be rewarded (11:8), though the word translated as *persistence* (or *importunity* in the RSV) is perhaps better rendered by *shamelessness*. It takes a certain kind of humility to beg this way, a certain disdain for human respect or the opinion of others. We should not let shame keep us from continuing to ask.

Jesus Teaches How to Ask in Prayer

Was Jesus shameless? Yes, shameless in emptying himself of his divinity, shameless in taking the form of a slave, shameless in accepting death—even death on a shameful cross (Phil 2:6–8). He was shameless in his need for continual prayer, and shameless in addressing God by the name *Abba*. It is also likely that he was shameless in asking for his most basic daily needs as he traveled with his disciples: the need for food and shelter. As Jesus says in setting out, ". . . the Son of man has nowhere to lay his head" (9:58). It is by asking God for these kinds of concrete things that the answers to our daily prayers can be verified daily. We can be certain that our shameless asking will not be met by a shameful failure on God's part to respond.

ENTERING INTO CONTEMPLATION

1. CHOOSE WHERE YOU WILL PRAY
   COMPOSE YOURSELF FOR PRAYER

Find a quiet place where you can be alone and uninterrupted for an hour. Take time to be still, to be present to God, and to express both your longing to know the mind and heart of Jesus and your desire to follow him more faithfully in your daily life.

"I TELL YOU, EVEN THOUGH HE WILL NOT GET UP AND GIVE HIM ANYTHING BECAUSE HE IS HIS FRIEND, AT LEAST BECAUSE OF HIS PERSISTANCE HE WILL GET UP AND GIVE HIM WHATEVER HE NEEDS."

AND HE SAID TO THEM, "SUPPOSE ONE OF YOU HAS A FRIEND. . . ."

2. IMAGINE THE SCENE

Having set his face, that is, made up his mind, to go to Jerusalem, the context for all that Jesus says and does in these succeeding chapters (9:51–18:14) is the journey with his companions to the Holy City. You might imagine yourself journeying with him and his disciples, sharing his total dependence on God, as they did when they were sent off carrying no money, no bread or clothing, no extra sandals (10:4). You might also picture yourself enduring with Jesus the poverty, the labors, the hunger and thirst, the heat and cold, the injuries and affronts that Ignatius mentions in the contemplation on the nativity (*Spiritual Exercises*, paragraph 116).

3. ASK FOR THIS GRACE

Jesus, draw me into the mystery of your shamelessness.

4. LISTEN TO WHAT THE PERSONS SAY

The disciples do not endure affronts very well when Samaritan villagers refuse to welcome them at the outset of this journey (9:53). With their new sense of power in the use of Jesus' name, James and John ask him, "Lord, do you want us to command fire to come down from heaven and consume them?" (9:54). They are confident that God will strike their enemies with lightning at their request! Jesus rebukes them, not for a misplaced confidence in the power of prayer, but for a prideful sense of themselves as miracle workers, and for a failure to understand both the mercy of God and Jesus' teaching on love of enemies (Lk 6:27–36). The parable is possibly preceded by some question to Jesus, such as, "Why is God so often slow to answer prayer?" Listen to the words Jesus speaks: "Suppose one of you has a friend . . ." This is an attempt to bring out the original meaning behind "Which of you shall have a friend . . ." (KJV). In other words, Jesus is saying, "Can you imagine a friend refusing to respond to your need in such a situation? Of course not!"

5. ENTER INTO CONVERSATION

Try to engage Jesus with your own response to this parable, a response coming out of your own experience of prayer to God for your needs. If you feel God has not listened to your prayer at times, say so, and see what Jesus says.

6. ENTER INTO SILENCE

You may have to struggle to understand or accept what Jesus says to you. Try to do so peacefully, pondering his words in your heart.

7. CONCLUSION

Thank Jesus for all that you have received in this prayer.

AFTER PRAYING

1. REFLECT ON THE EXPERIENCE

At the end of your contemplation, move to another place and spend a few minutes reviewing your experience of prayer, making note of those things that brought you either consolation or desolation, so that, if you do a repetition or application of the senses, you can return to them again, and enter more deeply into the mystery you are contemplating.

2. QUESTIONS THAT MAY ARISE OUT OF PRAYER

In difficult or desperate situations, would you turn to God? What would you ask for in prayer? How would you ask it of him? What quality would your prayer have? Does your discipleship—your daily life—demand a similar dependence on God to meet your needs as they arise? Does this require the same kind of prayer—the same kind of persistent, shameless begging?

"...Because of his persistance...."

What to Pray on Next

If you have done contemplations on both the above passages (in A and B), you can deepen your experience of prayer in the repetitions and application of senses. Otherwise, go on to one of the passages in C or D.

3. SEARCHING THE SCRIPTURES

In the Song of Solomon 5:2 (or the "Song of Songs" in some translations), we again find the image of knocking at the door:

> I slept, but my heart was awake.

> Listen! My beloved is knocking.

Christian tradition has long applied this beautiful series of love poems to Christ and his beloved spouse, the Church: Christ is the passionate lover who seeks a similar response of love from us. In the book of Revelation (3:20), the risen Christ says, "Listen! I am standing at the door, knocking. . . ." Here the roles are reversed, and it is Christ who stands outside, knocking at our door and calling to us to open. We may sometimes feel that God is slow to answer our prayers—we may even wonder whether God hears them. Is it possible that it is ourselves who are not listening to the one who shamelessly and persistently knocks at our door and calls us to let him into our life?

C. EFFECTIVE PRAYER: THE MYSTERY OF HIS TRUST

LUKE 11:9–13

1. Read the gospel passage slowly and carefully, seeking to understand it more deeply in its totality or in its parts as you wish.

2. Read the section Exploring the Gospel as an aid both to understanding the text and to stimulating your imagination when you pray.

3. Before you begin to pray, read the passage once again.

"So I say to you, Ask, and it will be given you; search, and you will find; knock, and the door will be opened for you. For everyone who asks receives, and everyone who searches finds, and for everyone who knocks, the door will be opened. Is there anyone among you who, if your child asks for a fish, will give a snake instead of a fish? Or if the child asks for an egg, will give a scorpion? If you then, who are evil, know how to give good gifts to your children, how much more will the heavenly Father give the Holy Spirit to those who ask him!" (9–13)

EXPLORING THE GOSPELS

Believing That Our Prayer Will Be Answered

Jesus continues his teaching on prayer by urging the disciples to be still more insistent—asking, searching, knocking—confident that their clamoring will be effective. For in prayer we are not just knocking at a neighbor's door in search of bread. We are calling upon our heavenly Father for our needs. An earthly father—even a bad father—will not deliberately give something harmful to a child who asks for food. What the heavenly Father will give is not just food for our sustenance but something much greater: the Holy Spirit!

Asking for What We Need

If God is eager to meet our needs, why should we ask at all? We ask because, first of all, in asking we *acknowledge* our need: we are not self-sufficient. In asking, we acknowledge also our *relationship* to God, not just as creatures but as children—as adopted children, yes, but as children having through Christ (Eph 1:5) the same relationship that Jesus has with God: we are those who can address God as *Abba*. In asking, then, we acknowledge this intimate relationship, and, in not giving up in spite of delays, we express our trust that God will indeed answer our prayer.

ENTERING INTO CONTEMPLATION

1. CHOOSE WHERE YOU WILL PRAY
COMPOSE YOURSELF FOR PRAYER

Find a quiet place where you can be alone and uninterrupted for an hour. Take time to be still, to be present to God, and to express both your longing to know the mind and heart of Jesus and your desire to follow him more faithfully in your daily life.

2. IMAGINE THE SCENE

Psalms 71 and 91 are only two of many psalms that sing of trust in God. Trust seems to be the most basic of all the virtues, closely related to hope and faith, and arising out of the childhood experience of being loved. Psalm 131:2 expresses beautifully this loving relationship with God, "But I have calmed and quieted my soul, like a weaned child with its mother. . . ." though it concludes with an exhortation to *hope* in its third and final verse:

"ASK, AND IT WILL BE GIVEN YOU; SEARCH, AND YOU WILL FIND; KNOCK, AND THE DOOR WILL BE OPENED FOR YOU."

O Israel, hope in the Lord from this time on and forevermore. It might just as well have used the word *trust* instead. Try to picture yourself as a child, secure in the comforting arms of your mother or father. Still and quiet your soul. Listen to your own breathing. Try to hear the pulsing of your heart. Love is all too often wounding. Can you trust in God's boundless love? What is it like to trust absolutely in God?

3.   ASK FOR THIS GRACE

Jesus, draw me into the mystery of your trust.

4.   LISTEN TO WHAT THE PERSONS SAY

"So I say to you . . ." Imagine Jesus addressing these words directly to you. He is urging real effort on your part: "Ask . . . search . . . knock . . ." Jesus speaks of asking for food—a fish and egg—but there are many other things that we may need and hunger for. With all our inadequacies and our sinfulness, our human hearts respond generously to the needs of children, especially our own children. We are God's own dear children, and God's heart is far more generous and responsive than ours.

5.   ENTER INTO CONVERSATION

Ask Jesus to teach you to trust. Tell him of your struggles to trust, and of the events that may have wounded your trust, especially of the wounds that came in childhood, when you were most vulnerable. You may not have been given a scorpion when you asked for an egg, but you may have been wounded in other ways. If you find yourself reliving childhood experiences, it may be helpful to speak to the child Jesus (picture him as being your own age). Or you may be drawn to Mary as to a mother who understands and comforts and brings healing. Speak whatever is in your heart—even anger, bitterness, hatred, violence. Try to get it all out.

"IF YOU THEN, WHO ARE EVIL, KNOW HOW TO GIVE GOOD GIFTS TO YOUR CHILDREN, HOW MUCH MORE WILL THE HEAVENLY FATHER GIVE THE HOLY SPIRIT TO THOSE WHO ASK HIM!"

6. ENTER INTO SILENCE

When you have emptied your heart of all your hurt and shed all your tears, calm and quiet your soul like a weaned child in Mary's arms (Ps 131:2) or in Jesus' arms. Enter into deep and quiet peace.

7. CONCLUSION

Thank Jesus for all that you have received in this prayer.

AFTER PRAYING

1. REFLECT ON THE EXPERIENCE

At the end of your contemplation, move to another place and spend a few minutes reviewing your experience of prayer, making note of those things that brought you either consolation or desolation, so that, if you do a repetition or application of the senses, you can return to them again, and enter more deeply into the mystery you are contemplating.

2. QUESTIONS THAT MAY ARISE OUT OF PRAYER

What should we ask for in prayer? And when should we ask? Is anything too petty, too selfish? In the *Spiritual Exercises*, Ignatius tells us at the start of each contemplation to ask for what we desire. We need to pray to *know* what it is that we really desire, since this is not always obvious. But usually our heart's desire is fairly clear. There are some desires that cannot be met immediately (for instance, that someone return to the Church, or that a friend be freed from an addiction, or that family members be reconciled to one another). But our most specific needs for each day are usually the ones to bring to prayer, and the best time to ask for help is as soon as we waken in the morning, even before we get out of bed, so that at the end of the day we can look back and see how our prayers have been answered.

> " FOR EVERYONE WHO ASKS RECEIVES, AND EVERYONE WHO SEARCHES FINDS, AND FOR EVERYONE WHO KNOCKS, THE DOOR WILL BE OPENED."

3. SEARCHING THE SCRIPTURES

Again and again the psalms give voice to our needs and desires, to our feelings and our faith (faith even in spite of how we may feel). Searching through the Psalter can often be an experience of being led by the Spirit to the text that best helps you to put your desires and needs into words. Most bibles have good headings for each psalm, but these vary from one version to another, so it may be helpful to have more than one version of the Bible at hand. A bible with cross-references in the margins can often make your search easier. The vision of the New Jerusalem (Rv 21:1–5) coming down out of heaven, adorned like a bride for her husband, is the ultimate answer to prayer, the fulfillment of all our hopes. The wedding feast of the bridegroom is the culmination of creation's coming into being—the fullness of creation, the fullness of being. God, who became one of us in taking on human flesh, will finally be fully at home among us, wiping away every tear from our eyes and making all things new.

What to Pray on Next

If you have completed two contemplations, do the repetitions and application of senses. If not, go on to the passage in section D.

114

Before You Pray

1. Read the gospel passage slowly and carefully, seeking to understand it more deeply in its totality or in its parts as you wish.

2. Read the section Exploring the Gospel as an aid both to understanding the text and to stimulating your imagination when you pray.

3. Before you begin to pray, read the passage once again.

D. CAREFREE PRAYER: THE MYSTERY OF HIS SERENITY

LUKE 12:22–32

He said to his disciples, "Therefore I tell you, do not worry about your life, what you will eat, or about your body, what you will wear. For life is more than food, and the body is more than clothing. Consider the ravens: they neither sow nor reap, they have neither storehouse nor barn, and yet God feeds them. Of how much more value are you than the birds! And can any of you by worrying add a single hour to your span of life? If then you are not able to do so small a thing as that, why do you worry about the rest? Consider the lilies, how they grow: they neither toil nor spin; yet I tell you, even Solomon in all his glory was not clothed like one of these. But if God so clothes the grass of the field, which is here today and tomorrow is thrown into the oven, how much more will he clothe you—you of little faith! And do not keep striving for what you are to eat and drink, and do not keep worrying. For it is the nations of the world that strive after all these things, and your Father knows that you need them. Instead, strive for his kingdom, and these things will be given to you as well." (12:22–32)

EXPLORING THE GOSPELS

Do Not Worry about Your Life

Anxiety is the child of mistrust. If we find ourselves anxious about the basic needs of life—food and clothing—it is because we do not trust God to provide these things, and we lack the faith to believe that God will in fact provide them. And so Jesus addresses some words of counsel to his disciples. Worrying about our life will not add to its length, he tells them, and anxiety about food and drink displays a poverty of faith that reduces his followers to the level of worldly people.

Consider the Ravens

The comparisons Jesus makes—with the common birds (the ravens) and plants (the lilies and the grass growing in the fields)—have to do primarily with God's loving care for these creatures. It is not that birds and animals are not concerned about food—it is almost their sole concern. And though ravens may not have barns and storehouses, other animals do store up food in certain seasons. But ultimately it is God who provides their food (12:24). And the beauty of the fields is God's gift as well (12:28). If God loves and cares for the least of creatures (the dry grass or straw that is burned in the oven each day for baking bread), how much more will God love and care for us—despite our lack of faith!

Strive for the Kingdom

Jesus does not tell the disciples that they should not work or that they should not pray for the basic necessities of life. He himself was once an artisan or craftsman who knows the meaning of work, and he has already taught them to say, "Father . . . Give us each day our daily bread" (11:2–3). He simply reminds them that their Father knows that they need all these things. And so, yes, ask! But do not be anxious. Trust that your prayers will be heard and answered, and do not worry. The

"THEREFORE I TELL YOU, DO NOT WORRY ABOUT YOUR LIFE, WHAT YOU WILL EAT, OR ABOUT YOUR BODY, WHAT YOU WILL WEAR. FOR LIFE IS MORE THAN FOOD, AND THE BODY IS MORE THAN CLOTHING."

one guiding principle that Jesus gives is this: strive for God's kingdom, and trust that all the other things will also be given (12:31). This again recalls the Lord's Prayer: "Your kingdom come" (11:2). And Jesus adds immediately, ". . . it is your Father's good pleasure to give you the kingdom" (12:32).

Keep Your Eyes on Jesus

In Galilee, Jesus and the Twelve were accompanied at times by various women "who provided for them out of their resources" (8:2–3). They did not have to worry about food and other necessities. Still, Jesus knew that it was God who met their needs through the generosity of Mary Magdalene and Joanna and others. It is God who continues to provide for them as they journey to Jerusalem. While the Twelve may have become anxious at times, it is hard to imagine Jesus as anything but serene and his prayer as anything but peaceful, trusting, and free from care.

ENTERING INTO CONTEMPLATION

1. CHOOSE WHERE YOU WILL PRAY
COMPOSE YOURSELF FOR PRAYER

Find a quiet place where you can be alone and uninterrupted for an hour. Take time to be still, to be present to God, and to express both your longing to know the mind and heart of Jesus and your desire to follow him more faithfully in your daily life.

2. IMAGINE THE SCENE

It is spring, and the hills at this time of year are green with grass. Include yourself among the disciples as they journey with Jesus along the Jordan Valley towards Jerusalem. Try to feel their anxiety as they approach dangerous or hostile territory.

"... STRIVE FOR HIS KINGDOM, AND THESE THINGS WILL BE GIVEN TO YOU AS WELL."

3. ASK FOR THIS GRACE

Jesus, draw me into the mystery of your serenity, your peace.

4. LISTEN TO WHAT THE PERSONS SAY

Listen to Jesus' words about God's providential care for all creatures. Imagine Jesus speaking directly to you when he says, "Of how much more value are you than the birds!" And again, "Do not be afraid . . ." (12:24, 32).

5. ENTER INTO CONVERSATION

Talk to Jesus about your cares and concerns, not only for yourself but also for those in your keeping. Observe how Jesus is concerned for his disciples and how he cares for their needs. If you are there as one of his disciples, try to see how he is concerned for *your* well-being and how much he cares for *you* and for your personal needs. Try to let go of all your anxiety, and try to abandon into the Father's hands all the things that you are most anxious about. Let the Spirit surround you and sustain you and fill you with peace.

6. ENTER INTO SILENCE

Enter into your own inner stillness—the stillness of your heart—and then into the stillness of Jesus' heart.

7. CONCLUSION

Thank Jesus for all that you have received in this prayer.

AFTER PRAYING

1. REFLECT ON THE EXPERIENCE

At the end of your contemplation, move to another place and spend a few minutes reviewing your experience of prayer, making note of those things that brought you either consolation or

"BUT IF GOD SO CLOTHES THE GRASS OF THE FIELD, WHICH IS HERE TODAY AND TOMORROW IS THROWN INTO THE OVEN, HOW MUCH MORE WILL HE CLOTHE YOU— YOU OF LITTLE FAITH!"

What to Pray on Next

Having come to the end of this fourth chapter, and having contemplated two of the passages above, you are ready to do the repetitions and end your day with the peaceful and passive appropriation of all that you have been given in prayer.

desolation, so that, if you do a repetition or application of the senses, you can return to them again, and enter more deeply into the mystery you are contemplating.

2. QUESTIONS THAT MAY ARISE OUT OF PRAYER

Can God really meet all my needs? Doesn't God help those who help themselves? Doesn't God expect us to make use of the things around us to meet our needs? In one of his letters, Ignatius writes:

> It is a mistake to rely upon oneself and so place one's hope in any resources or exertions for their own sake. Conversely, it is not a sure way to rely on God our Lord alone, without allowing myself to be helped by what he has given me. (*Ignatius the Theologian* by Hugh Rahner, S.J., 26)

The key phrase is "for their own sake." If our projects and works are done for God's sake, then we look to God for help and we leave their ultimate success or failure with God. We can pray and prepare for a project as though everything depends on us, which in some sense it does, and we can work and pray as though the success of everything depends on God, which ultimately it does.

3. SEARCHING THE SCRIPTURES

Jesus is teaching a wisdom that transcends our own. He *is* the Wisdom of God. The book of Proverbs presents us with some of Israel's most ancient attempts to discover God's wisdom in reflecting on human experience. The first nine chapters of Proverbs is a long series of reflections on what wisdom really is. The feeding of the five thousand in Luke 9:10–17 shows how deeply Jesus is concerned for peoples' basic needs, and how he manages to provide for them. Ignatius also teaches a kind of wisdom or discernment by having us reflect on our personal experience, whether it be the experience of our prayer or the experience of our day.

V.

JESUS'
TEACHING
ABOUT
PRAYER (2)

R ead the preparatory material below and choose two of the following passages for today's prayer.

A. *Thankful Prayer:*

   The Mystery of His Gratitude

   Luke 17:11–19

B. *Unceasing Prayer:*

   The Mystery of His Confidence

   Luke 18:1–8

C. *Humble Prayer:*

   The Mystery of His Mercy

   Luke 18:9–14

D. *Childlike Prayer:*

   The Mystery of His Simplicity

   Luke 18:15–17

T he word Abba implies a childlike simplicity in the one who prays the Lord's Prayer, and this remains Jesus' stance in all his prayer.

BACKGROUND

Jesus Continues His Instruction

Within the framework of the journey to Jerusalem with his chosen Twelve (9:51–19:27), Jesus continues to teach them through precept and parable.

The Importance of Gratitude

One of Jesus' instructional moments has to do with giving thanks. His ecstatic prayer that was referred to above (chapter III, section D) begins, "I thank you, Father . . ." (Lk 10:21). Though it is almost the only place in this gospel where Jesus gives thanks to God, apart from the Last Supper (22:17), we can imagine that thanksgiving was a normal part of his prayer. The Psalms, which were frequently on his lips, are filled with thanksgiving:

> O give thanks to the Lord, for he is good; for
> his steadfast love endures forever. (107:1)

Psalm 118 begins and ends with similar words, and is filled with expressions of gratitude for prayers heard and answered:

> I thank you that you have answered me and
> have become my salvation. (118:21)

Gratitude for past prayers heard and answered is what grounds our hope and trust that present and future prayers will meet with a similar reception and response.

Jesus Heals Ten Lepers

Jesus' single teaching on the need to give thanks (if it can be called a teaching) is found in the account of the ten lepers who were healed after being sent on their way to show themselves to the priests. Only one of them turned back to praise God and give thanks to Jesus, and this one was a "foreigner," a Samaritan. Although the account is of healing, of faith, and of salvation, the main point seems to be the thankfulness of the Samaritan. It is more than thanksgiving and gratitude, however, that moves the Samaritan. He is filled with wonder in his awareness of the gift of God, in his experience of the goodness and generosity of God, and this wonder turns to the praise and glorification of God. Ingratitude would seem to be the great sin of unbelievers, according to Paul, who tells us that "though they knew God, they did not honor him as God or give thanks to him" (Rom 1:21). Yet here the one excluded by Israel is the one who honors God and gives thanks.

Before You Pray

1. Read the gospel passage slowly and carefully, seeking to understand it more deeply in its totality or in its parts as you wish.

2. Read the section Exploring the Gospel as an aid both to understanding the text and to stimulating your imagination when you pray.

3. Before you begin to pray, read the passage once again.

A. THANKFUL PRAYER: THE MYSTERY OF HIS GRATITUDE

LUKE 17:11–19

On the way to Jerusalem Jesus was going through the region between Samaria and Galilee. As he entered a village, ten lepers approached him. Keeping their distance, they called out, saying, "Jesus, Master, have mercy on us!" When he saw them, he said to them, "Go, and show yourselves to the priests." And as they went, they were made clean. Then one of them, when he saw that he was healed, turned back, praising God with a loud voice. He prostrated himself at Jesus' feet and thanked him. And he was a Samaritan. Then Jesus asked, "Were not ten made clean? But the other nine, where are they? Was none of them found to return and give praise to God except this foreigner?" Then he said to him, "Get up and go on your way; your faith has made you well." (17:11–19)

EXPLORING THE GOSPELS

Jesus Is Moved to Compassion

Earlier in this gospel (10:29–37), in answer to the question, *Who is my neighbor?*, Jesus tells a parable in which a despised Samaritan is held up as an example of what it truly is to be a neighbor to someone in need. Now, a real-life Samaritan becomes a model of faith and gratitude. As he approaches a village, Jesus is met by ten lepers, who seem already to have heard of him. Keeping their distance, as required by the Law (Lv 13:45–46), they address him by name. They raise their voices to him in prayer, crying out, "Jesus, Master, have mercy on us!" Jesus does not heal them immediately, but sends them to the priests who were needed to verify any cure (the full ritual is described in Leviticus 14:1–32). With faith in Jesus' word, the ten lepers set out and on the way they are healed. One of them, a Samaritan, seeing that he was cured, returns praising God for this miraculous healing and thanks Jesus, the instrument of God's mercy. Jesus pointedly asks, "But the other nine, where are they?"

Jesus Is Touched by Gratitude

Though Jesus is obviously disappointed in the other nine, who presumably were his fellow countrymen, he is clearly touched by the faith and gratitude of the Samaritan, and is surely grateful in turn for this man's loud praise of God and for his humble gesture of thanksgiving. Gratitude, like joy, is contagious. If Jesus can give ecstatic thanks to the Father for revealing his saving power to the little ones who are his disciples (10:21), then he must also be moved with gratitude to God for opening the eyes of this humble Samaritan—this outcast among lepers—to recognize the mercy that has been shown him, and to see through whom this saving grace has come. It *is a saving* grace: the word translated as *made well* literally means *to save, to rescue from death*, as well as *to restore to health*, and is ultimately related to *salvation*.

ENTERING INTO CONTEMPLATION

1. CHOOSE WHERE YOU WILL PRAY
    COMPOSE YOURSELF FOR PRAYER

Find a quiet place where you can be alone and uninterrupted for an hour. Take time to be still, to be present to God, and to express both your longing to know the mind and heart of Jesus and your desire to follow him more faithfully in your daily life.

"GET UP AND GO ON YOUR WAY; YOUR FAITH HAS MADE YOU WELL."

Keeping their distance, they called out, saying, "Jesus, Master, have mercy on us!"

2. IMAGINE THE SCENE

Try to picture the lepers as they stand at a distance with their ragged clothing and disfigured flesh. You might begin this contemplation by putting yourself in the place of the Samaritan, who may have experienced rejection even from the other lepers. As a Samaritan, you would have had to show yourself to a Samaritan priest.

3. ASK FOR THIS GRACE

Jesus, draw me into the mystery of your gratitude.

4. LISTEN TO WHAT THE PERSONS SAY

As the lepers call out to Jesus, hear the pain and anguish in their voices. Hear also their hope. They recognize Jesus. They know his name. They have heard of his power to heal. Listen to Jesus' simple instructions and see their obedient response. What happens when you and your companions discover that you have been healed? We have no way of knowing what the other nine lepers experienced or felt. Perhaps some of them were so overcome with joy that they could think of nothing else than to have their cure verified as quickly as possible by the priests of their village. Whatever the other nine may have done, the one thing they did *not* do is return to Jesus and thank him.

5. ENTER INTO CONVERSATION

No doubt your village lies in a different direction from those of the other lepers, but instead of going to your home in Samaria, you turn around and come back to Jesus, throwing yourself down in the dust before him and thanking him. Express whatever is in your heart. Let him say what is in his heart.

6. ENTER INTO SILENCE

Try to understand how Jesus regards you and what gratitude he feels for *you*, and enter silently into mutual joy and gratitude for each other.

7. CONCLUSION

Thank Jesus for all that you have received in this prayer.

AFTER PRAYING

1. REFLECT ON THE EXPERIENCE

At the end of your contemplation, move to another place and spend a few minutes reviewing your experience of prayer, making note of those things that brought you either consolation or desolation, so that, if you do a repetition or application of the senses, you can return to them again, and enter more deeply into the mystery you are contemplating.

2. QUESTIONS THAT MAY ARISE OUT OF PRAYER

Ignatius Loyola is said to have considered ingratitude the worst possible sin. Why is ingratitude so sinful? How does gratitude situate us in relation to the gift? In relation to the giver? In relation to the giver of all gifts? What does it mean to truly appreciate a gift of any kind?

3. SEARCHING THE SCRIPTURES

In chapter 5 of the Second Book of Kings, we have the story of Naaman the Syrian, who is mentioned by Jesus in Luke 4:27. He is a mighty warrior, the commander of the army of the king of Aram, but he is a leper. Though he is a Gentile, he is healed of his leprosy by the prophet Elisha when he finally humbles himself to follow the prophet's instructions. His problem is pride

"WERE NOT TEN MADE CLEAN? BUT THE OTHER NINE, WHERE ARE THEY? WAS NONE OF THEM FOUND TO RETURN AND GIVE PRAISE TO GOD EXCEPT THIS FOREIGNER?"

What to Pray on Next

Go on to one of the following passages in B, C, or D.

and a preconceived notion of how a prophet should act. Upon being healed, he is filled not only with gratitude but also with faith: "Now I know that there is no God in all the earth except in Israel . . ." (5:15). Psalm 103 is a beautiful expression of gratitude for all that God has given, for all that God has done—forgiving, healing, redeeming. One could spend a whole retreat on this psalm alone, allowing one's heart to expand with gratitude and driving out all that is negative, all that is unworthy of a child of God.

B. UNCEASING PRAYER: THE MYSTERY OF HIS CONFIDENCE

LUKE 18:1–8

Then Jesus told them a parable about their need to pray always and not to lose heart. He said, "In a certain city there was a judge who neither feared God nor had respect for people. In that city there was a widow who kept coming to him and saying, 'Grant me justice against my opponent.' For a while he refused; but later he said to himself, 'Though I have no fear of God and no respect for anyone, yet because this widow keeps bothering me, I will grant her justice, so that she will not wear me out by continually coming.' " And the Lord said, "Listen to what the unjust judge says. And will not God grant justice to his chosen ones who cry to him day and night? Will he delay long in helping them? I tell you, he will quickly grant justice to them. And yet, when the Son of Man comes, will he find faith on earth?" (18:1–8)

Before You Pray

1. Read the gospel passage slowly and carefully, seeking to understand it more deeply in its totality or in its parts as you wish.

2. Read the section Exploring the Gospel as an aid both to understanding the text and to stimulating your imagination when you pray.

3. Before you begin to pray, read the passage once again.

"THOUGH I HAVE NO FEAR OF GOD AND NO RESPECT FOR ANYONE, YET BECAUSE THIS WIDOW KEEPS BOTHERING ME, I WILL GRANT HER JUSTICE, SO THAT SHE WILL NOT WEAR ME OUT BY CONTINUALLY COMING."

EXPLORING THE GOSPELS

The Persistent Widow

Here Jesus gives the disciples another parable about prayer. Like the parable about the neighbor who goes to a friend in the middle of the night to ask for bread (11:5-8), it seems to stress again the need for shameless persistence, though this time it is expressed as the need to pray always and not lose heart. The parable is usually called the "Parable of the Unjust Judge" and not the "Parable of the Persistent Widow," since the judge is the point of the parable, as Jesus himself makes clear. The widow does not give up her demands, but it is the judge who finally gives in to them. If such a despicable person, despite his dishonesty, can be persuaded to act justly, how much more surely will a loving and compassionate God grant justice to his chosen ones.

Another Way of Asking

These two parables are worth comparing. Each depicts a similar way of asking—one shamelessly and persistently, perhaps for many long minutes, the other continually, day after day, perhaps over many days. Besides the different time frames of the parables, each has a very different object of petition: one asks for bread, the other for justice. Some things, like bread, are easier to obtain than others, like justice. Though both parables may seem to require a change of heart on the part of the one being petitioned, it is a foregone conclusion that the bread will be obtained: because of the Near Eastern tradition of hospitality, not even a stranger would be refused such a thing as bread. For this reason the petitioning friend will be given what he needs in order to welcome his visitor. The judge, on the other hand, is unjust and cares for no one, not even for God. It is not at all certain that the widow will obtain what she asks. And yet, she does not give up. She keeps coming to him with her request, and eventually she succeeds.

Another Kind of Confidence

When we pray to God, "Give us each day our daily bread," we usually pray with confidence that it will be given that day. When we pray to God for something that will require a real change of heart on the part of another person, we have no way of knowing how long this will take, and yet we should still pray with confidence that our prayer will be answered. We should not lose confidence and give up because our prayer seems ineffectual.

Trusting That God Is at Work

When we pray that someone will regain a lost faith, or that a broken relationship will be restored, or that a loved one will be freed from addiction, we know that such things can take years, even a lifetime. Ultimately, we have to trust in the mercy of God, which is usually hidden from view. It is only in the life to come that we will finally see the full effect of our prayer. And yet we should still pray with confidence, knowing that God does indeed hear us and is already at work to answer our prayer in a way that we might not be able even to imagine. At the end of the fourth week of the *Spiritual Exercises*, we are asked to consider how God actually *works* and *labors* for us *in all created things* (paragraph 236), but we do this only after we have experienced the third week: the transformative mystery of Jesus' suffering and death on the cross. Only then can we begin to see God at work everywhere and in everything.

ENTERING INTO CONTEMPLATION

1. CHOOSE WHERE YOU WILL PRAY
   COMPOSE YOURSELF FOR PRAYER

Find a quiet place where you can be alone and uninterrupted for an hour. Take time to be still, to be present to God, and to express both your longing to know the mind and heart of Jesus and your desire to follow him more faithfully in your daily life.

"LISTEN TO WHAT THE UNJUST JUDGE SAYS. AND WILL NOT GOD GRANT JUSTICE TO HIS CHOSEN ONES WHO CRY TO HIM DAY AND NIGHT?"

> " I TELL YOU, HE WILL QUICKLY GRANT JUSTICE TO THEM. AND YET, WHEN THE SON OF MAN COMES, WILL HE FIND FAITH ON EARTH?"

2. IMAGINE THE SCENE

In contemplating this scene and in placing yourself among his disciples as Jesus teaches them about the need for unceasing prayer, you may find yourself asking why he is telling you this parable: what is it that he wants you to hear? In the preceding verses, Jesus has spoken to the disciples of the coming of the Son of Man: though the kingdom is already among them (as Jesus tells the Pharisees in 17:21), the disciples will long for the coming of the Son of Man and will not see it (17:22). And so they will need to pray with confidence for his return. What they will need is not just the confidence of the widow before the unjust judge, but the confident stance of Jesus himself in prayer before the Father.

3. ASK FOR THIS GRACE

Jesus, draw me into the mystery of your confidence.

4. LISTEN TO WHAT THE PERSONS SAY

What Jesus says, at least indirectly, is that his disciples will need to pray always and not lose heart. Listen also to his comparison of God to the judge: if even an unjust and unbelieving judge will acquiesce to the unceasing demands of a poor widow, how much more likely is their *Abba* to answer their prayers?

5. ENTER INTO CONVERSATION

The disciples' faith will be tested not only by God's delay in answering their prayers, but also by the scandal of Jesus' own suffering: "But first he [the Son of Man] must endure much suffering and be rejected by this generation" (17:25). Perhaps your own faith has been tested in similar ways. Perhaps it has been wounded by scandal. This is what needs to be talked about with Jesus.

6. ENTER INTO SILENCE

If Jesus insists on your need to pray always, it is only because he himself prays unceasingly. He is pleading silently for his disciples, for you. Still your heart with its struggling, quiet your mind with its questioning, and try to enter into Jesus' silent prayer.

7. CONCLUSION

Thank Jesus for all that you have received in this prayer.

AFTER PRAYING

1. REFLECT ON THE EXPERIENCE

At the end of your contemplation, move to another place and spend a few minutes reviewing your experience of prayer, making note of those things that brought you either consolation or desolation, so that, if you do a repetition or application of the senses, you can return to them again, and enter more deeply into the mystery you are contemplating.

2. QUESTIONS THAT MAY ARISE OUT OF PRAYER

Does Jesus want you to reflect on yourself in comparison to this widow? Does he want you to consider the desire that God has to speedily answer your prayers? Is justice something that can only be realized in the Second Coming? Finally, what about faith—your own faith in Jesus? Is it anything like his trust and confidence in the Father?

... THEIR NEED TO PRAY ALWAYS AND NOT TO LOSE HEART.

What to
Pray on Next

If you have done two contemplations using the texts in A and B, you are ready to move into the repetitions and the application of senses. If not, go on to one of the passages in C or D.

3. SEARCHING THE SCRIPTURES

It would be good to read what Moses says to his judges about impartiality (Dt 1:16–17), as well as what the prophets say about injustice—for instance, Jeremiah 22:13. Isaiah 9:6–7 looks forward to the coming of the Messiah to establish true justice. But most important are the words from the first chapter of Luke's other book: "This Jesus, who has been taken up from you into heaven, will come in the same way as you saw him go into heaven" (Acts 1:11).

C. HUMBLE PRAYER: THE MYSTERY OF HIS MERCY

LUKE 18:9–14

He also told this parable to some who trusted in themselves that they were righteous and regarded others with contempt. "Two men went up to the temple to pray, one a Pharisee and the other a tax collector. The Pharisee, standing by himself, was praying thus, 'God, I thank you that I am not like other people: thieves, rogues, adulterers, or even like this tax collector. I fast twice a week; I give a tenth of all my income.' But the tax collector, standing far off, would not even look up to heaven, but was beating his breast and saying, 'God, be merciful to me, a sinner!' I tell you, this man went down to his home justified rather than the other; for all who exalt themselves will be humbled, but all who humble themselves will be exalted." (9–14)

EXPLORING THE GOSPEL

The Pharisee and the Tax Collector

Jesus follows the Parable of the Unjust Judge with yet another parable: that of the Pharisee and the Tax Collector. This one is told not to the disciples but to people who were self-righteous and contemptuous of others—most likely, therefore, to Pharisees. It is worth noting that the Pharisee in this parable asks for nothing. He begins his prayer by thanking God. He is grateful

Before You Pray

1. Read the gospel passage slowly and carefully, seeking to understand it more deeply in its totality or in its parts as you wish.

2. Read the section Exploring the Gospel as an aid both to understanding the text and to stimulating your imagination when you pray.

3. Before you begin to pray, read the passage once again.

"GOD, I THANK YOU THAT I AM NOT LIKE OTHER PEOPLE: THIEVES, ROGUES, ADULTERERS, OR EVEN LIKE THIS TAX COLLECTOR."

for who he is and for what he is not, all of which is God's doing. He is conscious of the tax collector standing at some distance from him in the Temple courtyard, also at prayer, and he thanks God that he is not like him—not like someone who is hardly different from a thief.

The Pharisee Is Filled with Gratitude

Even what seems to be the Pharisee's boasting can be read as part of his thanksgiving: he thanks God that he is able to do so much more than the minimum required by the Law. Instead of fasting once a year (on the Day of Atonement), he fasts twice a week. He tithes all his income (literally: everything he buys)—perhaps even the garden herbs mentioned by Jesus in his condemnation of the Pharisees in Luke 11:42. In other words, he tithes not just the things stipulated by the Law. The form of this prayer is actually quite typical of the piety of the time, and its content is admirable in that it goes far beyond a legalistic minimalism. Anyone in attendance who overheard this man praying aloud must have felt that he was exemplary.

The Tax Collector Is Filled with Shame

In contrast, the tax collector, who is shunned by everyone with any self-respect, keeps his distance. This is not simply because he is a sinner, but because of the kind of sinner he is. He is a Jew employed by the Roman occupation as a gatherer of tolls (which included customs duties and indirect taxes)—already enough to make him despised by his fellow Jews as a traitor. The position of toll collector went to the highest bidder, who then had to recoup his money and make a profit as well. There were not many controls over how he did this, and toll collectors were universally loathed for growing rich by gouging excessive amounts from the poor. No wonder the Pharisee is grateful that he is not one of those.

The Tax Collector Is without Hope

For the tax collector to repent and change his sinful ways, however, he would not simply have to give up his business. Because his business involved theft, he would also have to make restitution. This meant, according to the Law, returning to each person wronged the amount owed plus one-fifth (Nm 5:7). It also required that he know exactly how much was owing and to whom—something of which he may not have had records. And so the tax collector sees no way out of his situation: it is hopeless. How shocking, then, for the Pharisees (and the disciples) to hear Jesus say that this dishonest man went home justified and not the other!

The Humility of God

It was with the Parable of the Prodigal Son (Lk 15:11–32) that Jesus responded to the Pharisees and scribes who criticized him earlier for welcoming tax collectors and sinners and for eating with them (15:1). That parable presents God as a loving and compassionate father, who, without regard for his dignity, runs to kiss his disgraced younger son, and then humbles himself still further to beg the older, self-righteous, Pharisaical one to come in and join the celebration. It is the truest, most beautiful image of God in all of scripture, and one that is mirrored frequently in the mercy shown to sinners by Jesus himself. It is the free gift of God's mercy that justifies people when they recognize their need for God, and not anything that even an upright person might do, however admirable.

The God of the Humble

In each of us there is something of the younger son and something of the older, something of the sinful tax collector and something of the self-righteous Pharisee. We cannot, any of us, see ourselves as we really are. Many of us have done things for which we could never make reparation. And yet we are known and understood and loved by God. What Jesus is saying is that, when we stand before God, who is humility itself, what counts most of all is our attitude. This is not to contradict what Jesus says elsewhere about the importance of love and of loving even our enemies (Lk 6:35), nor is it to contradict what Ignatius says in the *Spiritual Exercises* about love showing itself more in deeds than in words (paragraph 230). What Jesus means is that, in the final analysis, there is nothing we can do to win or earn God's love: it is pure gift.

"GOD, BE MERCIFUL TO ME, A SINNER!"

"SON, YOU HAVE ALWAYS BEEN WITH ME, AND ALL THAT IS MINE IS YOURS. BUT WE HAD TO CELEBRATE AND REJOICE, FOR THIS BROTHER OF YOURS WAS DEAD AND HAS BEGUN TO LIVE, AND WAS LOST AND HAS BEEN FOUND."

(LK 15:31–32)

The Humility of the Sinner

This is what the self-righteous cannot see. The older son cannot earn his father's love by obedience and hard work and by asking for nothing, nor can the Pharisee by all his praying and fasting and tithing. The younger son, in spite of (indeed because of) his reckless and sinful adventure, is able at last to humble himself by returning home and acknowledging that he is a sinner. The tax collector, in his despair of ever being able to rescue himself from his situation, is forced to throw himself on the compassion of God, saying humbly, "God, be merciful to me a sinner!" This attitude of humility—of humbly acknowledging the truth of what we are when left to ourselves—is what renders us acceptable and upright before God. Then God's love can cover a multitude of sins.

The Humility of the Disciple

The parable's concluding words can be read as addressed not just to those who trust in themselves or who hold others in contempt, but to all who wish to follow Jesus. Humility and mercy are embodied in everything that Jesus is and does. It is to be drawn into the mystery of that mercy upon mercy that you are asking now. If you wish, you could do this by using the "Jesus Prayer," which incorporates the words of the tax collector: "Jesus, Son of God and Savior, be merciful to me a sinner."

ENTERING INTO CONTEMPLATION

1. CHOOSE WHERE YOU WILL PRAY
   COMPOSE YOURSELF FOR PRAYER

Find a quiet place where you can be alone and uninterrupted for an hour. Take time to be still, to be present to God, and to express both your longing to know the mind and heart of Jesus and your desire to follow him more faithfully in your daily life.

2. IMAGINE THE SCENE

Try placing yourself in the position of one and then the other of these two persons, first the one who is very religious, generous, and grateful to God, and then the one who is trapped in a sinful situation without hope of being extricated. Ask yourself which you would really rather be, the Pharisee or the tax collector. Is it easier to live with the sense that one has God's mercy but doesn't seem to need it, or with the sense that one desperately needs God's mercy, but cannot see how it is possible to have it?

3. ASK FOR THIS GRACE

Jesus, draw me into the mystery of your mercy.

4. LISTEN TO WHAT THE PERSONS SAY

Try to listen on a deep level to what each of these persons is actually saying, and to identify with each in turn.

5. ENTER INTO CONVERSATION

Begin to speak separately to each person in this parable, trying to get to know each as a human being not all that different from yourself. Try to sympathize and empathize with each. Then talk to Jesus out of the depth of your own heart. What does he say back to you?

6. ENTER INTO SILENCE

You may find yourself caught in feelings that are difficult or painful to express. Ask for mercy, aloud or in silent pleading.

" . . . ALL WHO EXALT THEMSELVES WILL BE HUMBLED, BUT ALL WHO HUMBLE THEMSELVES WILL BE EXALTED."

7. CONCLUSION

Thank Jesus for all that you have received in this prayer.

AFTER PRAYING

1. REFLECT ON THE EXPERIENCE

At the end of your contemplation, move to another place and spend a few minutes reviewing your experience of prayer, making note of those things that brought you either consolation or desolation, so that, if you do a repetition or application of the senses, you can return to them again, and enter more deeply into the mystery you are contemplating.

2. QUESTIONS THAT MAY ARISE OUT OF PRAYER

Marxism has been called hope without faith. Is it possible to have faith without hope? Is despairing of oneself the same as being without hope? What is the difference between despairing of oneself and despairing of God? Is it necessary to become like the tax collector, that is, to despair of oneself, before being able to throw oneself entirely on the mercy of God? Is this similar to acknowledging one's powerlessness, as in the tradition of twelve step programs?

3. SEARCHING THE SCRIPTURES

Mercy is the message of the *Magnificat*, welcoming Jesus into the womb: "He has helped his servant Israel, in remembrance of his mercy" (1:54), as is also humility: "He has brought down the powerful from their thrones, and lifted up the lowly" (1:52). The opening words of Psalm 51 are what underlie the tax collector's prayer in Jesus' parable:

"BUT THE TAX COLLECTOR, STANDING FAR OFF, WOULD NOT EVEN LOOK UP TO HEAVEN, BUT WAS BEATING HIS BREAST. . . ."

Have mercy on me, O God, according to your steadfast love;

according to your abundant mercy blot out my transgressions.

Two actual tax collectors appear in Luke's gospel—Levi, elsewhere known as Matthew, whom Jesus calls to be a disciple (5:27–32), and Zacchaeus, one of the lost whom "the Son of Man came to seek out and to save" (19:1–10). Their situations seem quite different from that of the tax collector in the parable, but they too meet with mercy in encountering Jesus, who welcomes them into his company.

What to Pray on Next

If you have done contemplations on two of the passages, you are ready to do the repetitions and the application of senses. If not, go on to the passage in section D.

Before You Pray

1. Read the gospel passage slowly and carefully, seeking to understand it more deeply in its totality or in its parts as you wish.

2. Read the section Exploring the Gospel as an aid both to understanding the text and to stimulating your imagination when you pray.

3. Before you begin to pray, read the passage once again.

D. CHILDLIKE PRAYER: THE MYSTERY OF HIS SIMPLICITY

LUKE 18:15–17

People were bringing even infants to him that he might touch them, and when the disciples saw it, they sternly ordered them not to do it. But Jesus called for them and said, "Let the little children come to me, and do not stop them, for it is to such as these that the kingdom of God belongs. Truly I tell you, whoever does not receive the kingdom of God as a little child will never enter it." (15–17)

EXPLORING THE GOSPEL

Bringing Little Children to Jesus

The parable of the Pharisee and the tax collector, with its emphasis on humble prayer, is followed immediately by an incident in which the disciples try to prevent people from bringing little children, even infants, to Jesus for him to touch and probably lay his hands on them in blessing. In Matthew 19:13 we have an identical scene, and in the next verse (9:14) we have similar words: "For it is to such as these that the kingdom of heaven belongs." But we have to go back to Matthew 18:3 to find the words, "Truly I tell you, unless you change and become like little children, you will never enter the kingdom of heaven." Luke, however, stays with the wording of the parallel passage in Mark 10:13–16, which is significantly different: "Truly I tell you, whoever does not receive the kingdom of God as a little child will never enter it" (18:16).

Becoming Like Little Children

The focus of Matthew's passage is explicitly on humility. It continues with Jesus saying, "Whoever becomes humble like this little child is the greatest in the kingdom of heaven" (18:4). Luke's focus is no doubt also on humility, since the scene immediately follows the verse, ". . . for all who exalt themselves will be humbled, but all who humble themselves will be exalted" (18:14)—the concluding words of the parable of the Pharisee and the tax collector. But where Matthew's text simply tells us that we must change and become like little children, Luke's helps us to see more clearly *how* we are to do this: by *receiving* the kingdom as a little child. Jesus' words about how the kingdom of God is to be received are meant to teach us what is to be our habitual stance before God, in prayer as in everything else. Since a tiny child is not able to claim anything or to earn anything, to receive the kingdom as a little child is to receive it as sheer gift. It is to receive it with simplicity, with trust and with openness. It is, finally, to come before God as does Jesus himself, saying "Abba."

Receiving as a Little Child

To receive as a little child receives is usually easy enough when one *is* a little child. But how is an adult to do this? So much in our upbringing and in our culture urges us toward independence and self-reliance, toward accepting responsibility and taking control of our lives. Our identity is often tied in with the work we do and with what we earn, with our possessions and our achievements. Attitudes acquired over a lifetime need to be un-learned in order to put on the

"TRULY I TELL YOU, WHOEVER DOES NOT RECEIVE THE KINGDOM OF GOD AS A LITTLE CHILD WILL NEVER ENTER IT."

mind and heart of a child. This is not easily done, and yet this is what Jesus insists on here. Perhaps what we *can* try to do is to receive others the way Jesus receives these little children, and to receive him the way these little children receive him. To receive Jesus *is* to receive the kingdom. It is to allow the Triune God to dwell in us, to teach us and guide us.

ENTERING INTO CONTEMPLATION

1. CHOOSE WHERE YOU WILL PRAY
   COMPOSE YOURSELF FOR PRAYER

Find a quiet place where you can be alone and uninterrupted for an hour. Take time to be still, to be present to God, and to express both your longing to know the mind and heart of Jesus and your desire to follow him more faithfully in your daily life.

2. IMAGINE THE SCENE

Here the humble Jesus identifies on some deep level with these little children, inviting them to come to him, and invoking God's name over them. You might even imagine yourself as one of the little children whom Jesus calls to himself. Decide what age you will be—perhaps after you experienced your first deep hurt. See him welcome you into his embrace.

3. ASK FOR THIS GRACE

Jesus, draw me into the mystery of your childlike simplicity.

4. LISTEN TO WHAT THE PERSONS SAY

"Let the little children come to me." Jesus is inviting *you* to come to him. Perhaps he even speaks your name. Try not to resist his invitation. Listen to what he says as he prays aloud over you, "Abba, Father. . . ."

PEOPLE WERE BRINGING EVEN INFANTS TO HIM THAT HE MIGHT TOUCH THEM. . . .

5. ENTER INTO CONVERSATION

Let the child in you respond spontaneously. Look into Jesus' eyes. Tell him of your wounded heart. Allow him to lay his hands on your head. Let him hold you and love you and heal you. Let your joy express itself, and let your delight in Jesus mirror his delight in you. Whether your words come easily or haltingly, let them come.

6. ENTER INTO SILENCE

Rest secure in Jesus' arms. Let him hold you close. Be still.

7. CONCLUSION

Thank Jesus for all that you have received in this prayer.

AFTER PRAYING

1. REFLECT ON THE EXPERIENCE

At the end of your contemplation, move to another place and spend a few minutes reviewing your experience of prayer, making note of those things that brought you either consolation or desolation, so that, if you do a repetition or application of the senses, you can return to them again, and enter more deeply into the mystery you are contemplating.

2. QUESTIONS THAT MAY ARISE OUT OF PRAYER

How childlike is Jesus in his prayer? How is the kingdom present among the disciples? How is the kingdom present among us? How have you received it? What does it mean to say that Jesus is the kingdom? Does Jesus have a sentimental attitude toward children? Does he love them and welcome them because they are tiny and innocent, or because they are vulnerable and wounded in some way by life?

"LET THE LITTLE CHILDREN COME TO ME, AND DO NOT STOP THEM, FOR IT IS TO SUCH AS THESE THAT THE KINGDOM OF GOD BELONGS."

What to Pray on Next

You have come to the end of the fifth chapter, your fifth day of retreat (unless you are doing these contemplations in the midst of your daily life). Having prayed over two of the passages provided above, you are ready to reflect on your experiences of prayer this day, deepening them in the repetitions and appropriating in the application of senses the graces you have received.

3. SEARCHING THE SCRIPTURES

Psalm 127:3 speaks of children ("the fruit of the womb") as a reward from God, and Psalm 128:3 describes them as being "like olive shoots around your table," a blessing from God. In 1 Corinthians 13:11, Paul says, "When I was a child, I spoke like a child, I thought like a child, I reasoned like a child; when I became an adult I put an end to childish ways." Does this contradict what Jesus says about becoming a child or receiving the kingdom as a little child?

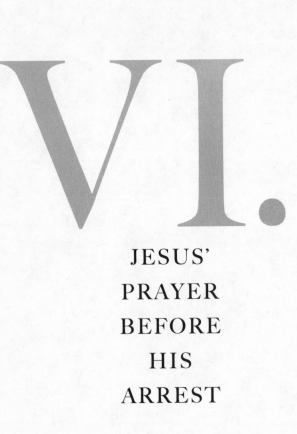

VI.

JESUS' PRAYER BEFORE HIS ARREST

Read the preparatory material below and choose two of the following passages for today's prayer.

    A.   *Preparation and Desire:*

          The Mystery of His Longing

          Luke 22:7–16

    B.   *The Last Supper:*

          The Mystery of His Eucharist

          Luke 22:17–23

    C.   *Peter's Denial Predicted:*

          The Mystery of His Prayer for Peter

          Luke 22:31–34

    D.   *Prayer on the Mount of Olives:*

          The Mystery of His Agony

          Luke 22:39–46

Jesus' life and prayer, his lived communion with the Father in the Spirit, have combined to bring him to the moment when the drama of his passion begins.

BACKGROUND

Jesus' Ministry in Jerusalem

The journey to Jerusalem culminates in Jesus' royal entry into the Holy City (Lk 19:28–40). His cleansing of the Temple courtyard shortly afterward (19:45–46) is an attack on the chief priests whose domain it is, and, together with the scribes and elders, they challenge Jesus' authority for doing such things (20:1–8). His ministry in Jerusalem, which takes up two-and-a-half chapters in this gospel, concludes with Luke's brief summary: "Every day he was teaching in the temple, and at night he would go out and spend the night on the Mount of Olives, as it was called. And all the people would get up early in the morning to listen to him in the temple" (21:37–38). During this period, Jesus and his disciples spend their days in the Temple courtyard and their nights not in the city, but just outside it, in the olive groves on the other side of the Kidron Valley (mentioned in John 18:1).

Jesus' Nights Spent in Prayer

From what we have seen of Jesus' penchant for praying at nighttime, it is likely that a good part of each night on the Mount of Olives was spent in prayer, alone or with his disciples—all the more intensely, considering that the Passion he predicted is now imminent. The Passion Narrative (22:1–23:56a) marks a shift in Jesus' prayer. The celebration of the Last Supper with the apostles is a different form of prayer, and leads to a long farewell discourse by Jesus. It is followed by his final prayer on the Mount of Olives, just before his betrayal by Judas Iscariot and his apprehension by the chief priests, temple officers, and elders.

The Conspiracy Against Jesus

As the festival of unleavened bread draws near (22:1), Judas conspires with the chief priests and temple authorities to hand Jesus over to them (22:2–6). Though Jesus has seen Satan fall like lightning from heaven (Lk 10:18), the enemy is still at work. Here Satan is named again as part of this conspiracy, "having entered into Judas called Iscariot" (22:3). Meanwhile, Jesus sends Peter and John into the city to prepare the Passover meal.

Before You Pray

1. Read the gospel passage slowly and carefully, seeking to understand it more deeply in its totality or in its parts as you wish.

2. Read the section Exploring the Gospel as an aid both to understanding the text and to stimulating your imagination when you pray.

3. Before you begin to pray, read the passage once again.

A. PREPARATION AND DESIRE: THE MYSTERY OF HIS LONGING

LUKE 22:7–16

Then came the day of unleavened bread, on which the Passover lamb had to be sacrificed. So Jesus sent Peter and John, saying, "Go and prepare the Passover meal for us that we may eat it." They asked him, "Where do you want us to make preparations for it?" "Listen," he said to them, "when you have entered the city, a man carrying a jar of water will meet you; follow him into the house he enters and say to the owner of the house, 'The teacher asks you, "Where is the guest room, where I may eat the Passover with my disciples?"' He will show you a large room upstairs, already furnished. Make preparations for us there." So they went and found everything as he had told them; and they prepared the Passover meal. (22:7–13)

When the hour came, he took his place at the table, and the apostles with him. He said to them, "I have eagerly desired to eat this Passover with you before I suffer; for I tell you, I will not eat it until it is fulfilled in the kingdom of God." (14–16)

EXPLORING THE GOSPEL

The Passover Meal

Luke, like Mark and Matthew, mentions only a single Passover in his gospel, whereas John's gospel mentions three separate Passover festivals. The "Last Supper," as it has come to be known, is the Passover that Jesus celebrates with his disciples as the prelude to his death on the cross, a Passover that he says he greatly desires to share with them. The Passover meal that he celebrates in Jerusalem would be one that Jesus presides over as head of his surrogate family of disciples, represented by its inner circle, the Twelve.

A Liturgical Prayer

This ritual meal is an extended liturgical prayer involving many blessings—over the feast, over the three servings of wine, and over the various symbolic foods. It would involve a retelling of the story of the Exodus from Egypt on the night of the first Passover, and the singing of Psalms (probably 113 and 114 at the beginning of the meal and 115 to 118 at the end). The central part of this sacred meal would be the blessing over the unleavened bread and the eating of the Passover lamb with bitter herbs, followed by the "cup of blessing"—the third and final cup of wine.

Exodus and the Kingdom

The Passover meal in Jesus' day was both a present *re-living* of the past (that is, of the Exodus experience of liberation) and an anticipation of the future (that is, of the liberation hoped for in the coming of the Messiah). This messianic longing is expressed in the words of Psalm 118:26—"Blessed is the one who comes in the name of the Lord"—which was shouted earlier during Jesus' triumphant entry into Jerusalem: "Blessed is the king who comes in the name of the Lord" (Lk 19:38). Now Jesus speaks again about the coming of the kingdom: He will not eat any more

THEN CAME THE DAY OF UNLEAVENED BREAD, ON WHICH THE PASSOVER LAMB HAD TO BE SACRIFICED.

Passover meals until this one is fulfilled in the kingdom of God—until the kingdom of God comes. And yet, as he said earlier, ". . . the kingdom of God is near" (21:31), and ". . . the kingdom of God is among you" (Luke 17:21). Here, in *this* Passover meal, both Israel's and Jesus' longing for the kingdom come together, as past and future, Exodus and the kingdom, meet in the present.

ENTERING INTO CONTEMPLATION

1. CHOOSE WHERE YOU WILL PRAY
COMPOSE YOURSELF FOR PRAYER

Find a quiet place where you can be alone and uninterrupted for an hour. Take time to be still, to be present to God, and to express both your longing to know the mind and heart of Jesus and your desire to follow him more faithfully in your daily life.

2. IMAGINE THE SCENE

Try to imagine yourself present at this Passover meal, reclining with the others on cushions around a low, central table. You are there either as one of the Twelve or as a beloved disciple, in a way that is attentive to what Jesus is experiencing, sensitive to what is going on in his heart. Try to build on all that you have been graced with so far in your previous contemplations, so that you can deepen your own desire. Desire is the key to prayer—yours and his. It is the key to Ignatian prayer, repeated over and over again in the *Spiritual Exercises*: ". . . to ask for what I desire . . . to ask for what I want. . . ." Undying desire is the key to the continuous, unceasing prayer that Paul urges (1 Thes 5:17). Ask this desire for yourself. Ask with all your heart to be drawn into the mystery of Jesus' desire, into the mystery of Jesus' longing—his longing for the whole of creation, his longing for every person, his ardent longing for you.

" I HAVE EAGERLY DESIRED TO EAT THIS PASSOVER WITH YOU BEFORE I SUFFER. . . ."

3. ASK FOR THIS GRACE

Jesus, draw me into the mystery of your longing.

4. LISTEN TO WHAT THE PERSONS SAY

The first words of Jesus at the Passover meal, as Luke gives them (22:15), translated literally, are, "With desire I have desired to eat this Passover with you before I suffer" (as in the Authorized or King James Version). This doubling of the word *desire* is a way of intensifying it in both Greek and Aramaic, and its quality is perhaps best captured in English by the word *longing*: "With all my heart I have longed to eat this Passover with you . . ." (J.B. Philipps), and in French by the word *ardeur*: *"J'ai désiré avec ardeur manger cette Pâques avec vous . . ." (La Bible de Jérusalem)*. It is this deep, ardent, and intense desire that you in turn are longing to enter into, so that your longing and his may become one.

5. ENTER INTO CONVERSATION

What do you want to say to Jesus in this sacred moment? Remember that you are there as a beloved companion, an intimate friend. What is your deepest desire, what is the ardent longing of your heart as you find yourself there with Jesus?

6. ENTER INTO SILENCE

If you find yourself without words, so much the better. Simply be present to Jesus, be close to him, close to his heart.

7. CONCLUSION

Thank Jesus for all that you have received in this prayer.

"... FOR I TELL YOU, I WILL NOT EAT IT UNTIL IT IS FULFILLED IN THE KINGDOM OF GOD."

What to
Pray on Next

Go on to one of the passages in sections B, C, or D.

AFTER PRAYING

1.   REFLECT ON THE EXPERIENCE

At the end of your contemplation, move to another place and spend a few minutes reviewing your experience of prayer, making note of those things that brought you either consolation or desolation, so that, if you do a repetition or application of the senses, you can return to them again, and enter more deeply into the mystery you are contemplating.

2.   QUESTIONS THAT MAY ARISE OUT OF PRAYER

What does Jesus' desire reveal to you about the love and longing of the Trinity? What does it tell you of God's infinite love for you? Does it call forth a similar, corresponding desire in you?

3.   SEARCHING THE SCRIPTURES

The steadfast love of God is sung in many of the psalms, as it is in Psalm 103. Psalm 42 pours out the longing of one's soul for God, as does Psalm 63.

B. THE LAST SUPPER: THE MYSTERY OF HIS EUCHARIST

LUKE 22:17–23

Before You Pray

1. Read the gospel passage slowly and carefully, seeking to understand it more deeply in its totality or in its parts as you wish.

2. Read the section Exploring the Gospel as an aid both to understanding the text and to stimulating your imagination when you pray.

3. Before you begin to pray, read the passage once again.

Then he took a cup, and after giving thanks, he said, "Take this and divide it among yourselves; for I tell you that from now on I will not drink of the fruit of the vine until the kingdom of God comes." Then he took a loaf of bread, and when he had given thanks, he broke it and gave it to them, saying, "This is my body, which is given for you. Do this in remembrance of me." And he did the same with the cup after supper, saying, "This cup that is poured out for you is the new covenant in my blood. But see, the one who betrays me is with me, and his hand is on the table. For the Son of Man is going as it has been determined, but woe to the one by whom he is betrayed!" Then they began to ask one another which one of them it could be who would do this. (17–23)

" ... **F**OR I TELL YOU THAT FROM NOW ON I WILL NOT DRINK OF THE FRUIT OF THE VINE UNTIL THE KINGDOM OF GOD COMES."

EXPLORING THE GOSPEL

A Change in Meaning

Jesus does more than celebrate another longed for and final Passover meal at what has come to be called the "Last Supper." In changing the words of blessing over the unleavened Passover bread and over the final cup of wine, he changes the meaning of the meal. The blessing that Jesus pronounces is expressed in the gospel by a Greek word from which we derive the word *Eucharist*, meaning *thanksgiving, thankfulness,* or *gratitude*. Instead of recalling the "bread of affliction" that was eaten at the first Passover (Dt 16:3), Jesus says, "This is my body which is given for you"—he is going to his death. And he adds, "Do this in remembrance of me," which is not found in Matthew or Mark (though it is found in 1 Corinthians 11:24). Whether or not Jesus actually spoke this directive, it is clear that the disciples understood from his actions that, from now on, they are to celebrate—to remember and relive—*his* Passover, *his* Exodus. It will be called the "Lord's Supper" by Paul (1 Cor 11:20), and later the "Eucharist."

The Cup of Blessing

In his account, Luke preserves traces of the Passover meal, mentioning two cups of wine. Of the three ritual cups of wine that traditionally are drunk at the meal, he mentions a first cup that Jesus shares with the Twelve (22:17), again saying that he will not drink wine (that is, Passover wine) again until the coming of the kingdom. But it is the final cup whose meaning is changed— "the cup after supper" (22:20), that is, the cup of blessing. Paul uses both phrases in his account of the early Christian community's Eucharistic practice: "The cup of blessing that we bless, is it not a sharing in the blood of Christ?" (1 Cor 10:16), and "In the same way he took the cup also, *after supper*, saying, 'This cup is the new covenant in my blood'" (1 Cor 11:25, emphasis mine). Luke's version is, "And he did the same with the cup after supper, saying, 'This cup that is poured out for you is the new covenant in my blood.'"

Jesus' Coming Death

Jesus' words about his body being "given for you" and about the cup of his blood "that is poured out for you" all point to his approaching death. His death is being given meaning by this new Passover meal, and the meal itself is being given meaning in the light of his imminent death. This meaning will become clear only after Jesus' resurrection, when he is recognized by the disciples at Emmaus in "the breaking of the Bread" (Lk 24:30–35).

ENTERING INTO CONTEMPLATION

1. CHOOSE WHERE YOU WILL PRAY
    COMPOSE YOURSELF FOR PRAYER

Find a quiet place where you can be alone and uninterrupted for an hour. Take time to be still, to be present to God, and to express both your longing to know the mind and heart of Jesus and your desire to follow him more faithfully in your daily life.

2. IMAGINE THE SCENE

As one of his present-day disciples, you can again place yourself in imagination at the Last Supper. Make Jesus the focus of your whole attention. See him bless, break, and share the unleavened bread. See him bless and share the cup. Hear his words. Try to feel what he is feeling—his desire to prepare the disciples for what is coming, his clarity about it, even about his betrayer. In the *Spiritual Exercises*, Ignatius says to consider how the divinity of Jesus hides itself in his humanity (paragraph 196). He remains totally human, totally vulnerable. Allow his gaze to meet yours. He sees you just as you are, he knows you as you are, he loves you as you are. All that he is about to do he does for the world, but he does it also for you, as though for you alone.

"FOR THE SON OF MAN IS GOING AS IT HAS BEEN DETERMINED. . . ."

"THIS IS MY BODY,
WHICH IS GIVEN
FOR YOU."

"THIS CUP THAT IS
POURED OUT FOR
YOU IS THE NEW
COVENANT IN MY
BLOOD."

3. ASK FOR THIS GRACE

Jesus, draw me into the mystery of your Eucharist.

4. LISTEN TO WHAT THE PERSONS SAY

"This is my body which is given for you." The disciples could not really understand all that Jesus means by these words, but you can bring to your prayer all that you understand of the Eucharist.

"This cup that is poured out for you is the new covenant in my blood." The disciples would be familiar with the blood of the Temple sacrifices and with the blood of the Passover lamb. You can bring to your prayer all that you understand of the New Covenant as well as the Eucharist.

5. ENTER INTO CONVERSATION

This is a moment of great mystery. You are being invited into the most intimate communion with Jesus, into his communion with the Father and with the whole created cosmos. How do you express what you are feeling at this moment?

6. ENTER INTO SILENCE

Try not to say too much. Just be present.

7. CONCLUSION

Thank Jesus for all that you have received in this prayer.

AFTER PRAYING

1. REFLECT ON THE EXPERIENCE

At the end of your contemplation, move to another place and spend a few minutes reviewing your experience of prayer, making note of those things that brought you either consolation or desolation, so that, if you do a repetition or application of the senses, you can return to them again, and enter more deeply into the mystery you are contemplating.

2. QUESTIONS THAT MAY ARISE OUT OF PRAYER

The mystery of the Eucharist is the mystery of Jesus' presence, not just in bread and wine but also in the power of his word spoken over bread and wine. Is his presence in the bread and wine of the Last Supper (before his death and resurrection) different from his presence in the breaking of bread celebrated by his disciples after the resurrection? The mystery of the Eucharist is also the mystery of Jesus' presence in the community of disciples that gathers in his name to proclaim the gospel and to break the bread, especially on the first day of the week, the day of his resurrection. The Eucharist is a mystery that has its full meaning only in the context of the resurrection and of Jesus' abiding presence in the community of his disciples.

3. SEARCHING THE SCRIPTURES

The Passover meal has its origins in the Exodus of Israel from Egypt as a memorial of the greatest event in Israel's history. Exodus 12:1–13 gives the ritual of the Passover lamb and unleavened bread, found also in Deuteronomy 16:1–8. The meal itself was elaborated over the centuries, but retained its essential meaning of Israel's liberation by God from bondage.

What to Pray on Next

If you have contemplated both the passages above in A and B, you are ready to do the repetitions and the application of senses, otherwise move on to one of the passages in sections C or D.

158

Before You Pray

1. Read the gospel passage slowly and carefully, seeking to understand it more deeply in its totality or in its parts as you wish.

2. Read the section Exploring the Gospel as an aid both to understanding the text and to stimulating your imagination when you pray.

3. Before you begin to pray, read the passage once again.

C. PETER'S DENIAL PREDICTED: THE MYSTERY OF HIS PRAYER FOR PETER

LUKE 22:31-34

"Simon, Simon, Listen! Satan has demanded to sift all of you like wheat, but I have prayed for you that your faith may not fail; and you, when once you have turned back, strengthen your brothers." And he said to him, "Lord, I am ready to go with you to prison and to death!" Jesus said, "I tell you, Peter, the cock will not crow this day, until you have denied three times that you know me." (31–34)

EXPLORING THE GOSPEL

Jesus Is There Serving Them

After the confusion that erupts around the question of which of them is going to betray Jesus, there is further confusion created in a dispute about which of them is the greatest (22:24–30). Jesus tells them that this is the kind of thing that pagans are concerned with. Greatness for them is to be found in humility—in being like the youngest or least important. Leadership with them is to be found in service—in being like Jesus, who is among them as one who serves (22:26). This would seem to imply that Jesus himself is serving them at the Passover meal. These words are not found in Matthew's and Mark's accounts of the Last Supper (Jesus has no farewell discourse in them). Perhaps, like the foot-washing account in John's gospel, these words indicate that Jesus is giving the Twelve an example of humble service to be imitated in their life as a community of disciples and in their ministry to others. They are the ones, Jesus continues, who have stood by him in his trials (22:28). He promises that one day they will eat and drink at his table in his kingdom, and even sit on thrones as judges (22:29–30).

Peter Is About to Deny Jesus

Having already mentioned that one of the Twelve is even now betraying him (22:21), Jesus proceeds to address some painful words to all of them and, in particular, to Peter. Though Luke does not depict the Twelve as deserting Jesus, he does have Jesus warn them that Satan will test them. Luke does not often show Peter in a harsh light (for instance, in this gospel, Peter does not rebuke Jesus after the first prediction of the Passion, and so Jesus is not shown rebuking him with the words, "Get behind me, Satan!"). But Peter's denial of Jesus is too well known to be omitted. Indeed, it shows that Peter, for all his giftedness and good will, is, like everyone else, weak and sinful. Yet Jesus' prayer will restore him. The repetition of Peter's given name, "Simon, Simon," indicates the importance of what Jesus is about to say. In many places in the scriptures, the repetition of a name indicates a vocation narrative, for instance, "Samuel, Samuel" (in 1 Samuel 3:1–21) or "Saul, Saul" (in Luke's other book, the Acts of the Apostles, 9:1–22). Though this is not strictly such a vocation or calling, Jesus does say that Peter will have a new and special role in strengthening the faith and fidelity of others in the community after he has been humbled by his own infidelity.

"I TELL YOU, PETER, THE COCK WILL NOT CROW THIS DAY, UNTIL YOU HAVE DENIED THREE TIMES THAT YOU KNOW ME."

"... I HAVE PRAYED FOR YOU THAT YOUR FAITH MAY NOT FAIL. . . ."

Jesus Is About to Die

Behind Jesus' words is the awareness that his death is imminent. Jesus has not arrived at this point by chance. He has deliberately chosen to challenge the authority of those who distort the Law of Moses—for instance, in his woes against the Pharisees and the scribes or lawyers, who then lie in wait to entrap him (Lk 11:42–54). He has also challenged those with religious-political power, that is, the chief priests, whose complicity with the Roman occupation involves them in the oppression of the poor. He did this especially in his cleansing of the Temple courtyard (Lk 19:45–48). He foresees that "this generation will be charged with the blood of all the prophets shed since the foundation of the world" (Lk 11:50), and thus identifies himself with these prophets.

Jesus Prays for Peter

In the *Spiritual Exercises*, Ignatius says that "the enemy of human nature" operates like a military tactician: he examines our defenses and, where he finds us weakest, there he attacks, hoping to capture us (paragraph 327). The evil spirit is at work, not only in Judas Iscariot but in all of the Twelve, to test them in order to see what they are really made of. Though Jesus says, "I have prayed for you"—that is, for Peter (*you* here is singular, as shown in the Authorized or King James Version by the use of *thee*)—we can be sure that he has prayed for all of them, including Judas. But it is for Peter in particular that he has prayed, because of Peter's assigned leadership. Peter will betray Jesus—not in a premeditated way, like Judas, but out of weakness and fear. Luke may even soften Jesus' words a little here, having him say, not "You will deny *me*" (as in Mark 14:30), but will have "denied . . . that you *know* me." Still, this is what Jesus predicts that Peter will do, even though Peter protests that he is ready and willing to die for Jesus.

ENTERING INTO PRAYER

1. CHOOSE WHERE YOU WILL PRAY
COMPOSE YOURSELF FOR PRAYER

Find a quiet place where you can be alone and uninterrupted for an hour. Take time to be still, to be present to God, and to express both your longing to know the mind and heart of Jesus and your desire to follow him more faithfully in your daily life.

2. IMAGINE THE SCENE

In your contemplation of this scene, you may want to put yourself in the place of Peter. But try especially to imagine what Jesus is feeling at this moment. His longing to share this Passover meal with his closest disciples is surely suffused with sadness at the thought of his betrayal—especially his denial by Peter. Try to sense the love that Jesus has for each of them, even for Judas, but especially for Peter. See his vulnerability and his defenselessness in the face of all the forces being marshalled against him: behind Judas, the chief priests of the Temple; behind the chief priests, Pontius Pilate; behind Pilate, the Roman emperor who appointed him; and behind all of them, the evil spirit by whom Jesus was tested during his forty days in the wilderness.

3. ASK FOR THIS GRACE

Jesus, draw me into the mystery of your prayer for Peter.

4. LISTEN TO WHAT THE PERSONS SAY

Jesus has prayed—is praying—for Peter. He will let Peter deny him, just as he lets Judas betray him. He sees that they will wound themselves as well as him in their betrayal and denial, and yet he lets them do all this because he loves them. His prayer has power to save—to save even Judas. Peter's readiness to go to prison and to death expresses his great devotion to Jesus, and yet, as Jesus foretells, Peter will deny him.

"SATAN HAS DEMANDED TO SIFT ALL OF YOU LIKE WHEAT. . . ."

"LORD, I AM READY TO GO WITH YOU TO PRISON AND TO DEATH!"

5. ENTER INTO CONVERSATION

Jesus is praying now also for you. He lets you do the things you do—even the hurtful things—because he loves you. His prayer is powerful and can call you back to yourself, and back to him. Perhaps, like Peter, you cannot foresee much that the future holds, but you can look back on the past and be attentive in the present. Try to see all that Jesus has done and is doing for you. How do you respond?

6. ENTER INTO SILENCE

When you have poured out all that is in your heart, knowing that there is so much more that you can never express in words, let the quiet presence of Jesus enfold you in his peace.

7. CONCLUSION

Thank Jesus for all that you have received in this prayer.

AFTER PRAYING

1. REFLECT ON THE EXPERIENCE

At the end of your contemplation, move to another place and spend a few minutes reviewing your experience of prayer, making note of those things that brought you either consolation or desolation, so that, if you do a repetition or application of the senses, you can return to them again, and enter more deeply into the mystery you are contemplating.

2. QUESTIONS THAT MAY ARISE OUT OF PRAYER

Ignatius says that "love ought to show itself more in deeds than in words" (*Spiritual Exercises*, paragraph 230). Does this mean that words are not important in expressing love? Are Peter's words about going to prison and to death expressive of genuine love or is he merely being rash? If Peter's love for Jesus is genuine, what does he still lack?

3. SEARCHING THE SCRIPTURES

The story of King David's adultery with Bathsheba and his subsequent murder of her husband (2 Sm 11:1–12:25) is a story of betrayal on many levels, and yet David, after being confronted by the prophet Nathan, finds forgiveness and reconciliation, though he must live with the consequences of his actions. The betrayal of the Son of David is very different, leading to Jesus' Crucifixion, yet it too can find forgiveness.

*What to
Pray on Next*

If you have done contemplations on two of the passages above, do the repetitions and the application of senses. If not, go on to the passage in D.

Before You Pray

1. Read the gospel passage slowly and carefully, seeking to understand it more deeply in its totality or in its parts as you wish.

2. Read the section Exploring the Gospel as an aid both to understanding the text and to stimulating your imagination when you pray.

3. Before you begin to pray, read the passage once again.

D. PRAYER ON THE MOUNT OF OLIVES: THE MYSTERY OF HIS AGONY

LUKE 22:39–46

He came out and went, as was his custom, to the Mount of Olives; and the disciples followed him. When he reached the place, he said to them, "Pray that you may not come into the time of trial." Then he withdrew from them, about a stone's throw, knelt down, and prayed, "Father, if you are willing, remove this cup from me; yet, not my will but yours be done." Then an angel from heaven appeared to him and gave him strength. In his anguish he prayed more earnestly, and his sweat became like great drops of blood falling down on the ground. When he got up from prayer, he came to the disciples and found them sleeping because of grief, and he said to them, "Why are you sleeping? Get up and pray that you may not come into the time of trial." (39–46)

EXPLORING THE GOSPEL

Jesus Goes to the Mount of Olives

Jesus concludes his discourse at the Last Supper by urging the Twelve to be prepared for the coming crisis. He quotes Isaiah (53:12), "And he was counted among the lawless," saying that this scripture must be—indeed, is being—fulfilled in him. Then he goes, "as was his custom," to the Mount of Olives. The disciples follow, and, though none of them is named, we can assume that all but Judas Iscariot go with him. Judas, of course, is quite familiar with the place to which Jesus normally retires for the night.

Jesus Tells His Disciples to Pray

Luke's account of Jesus' prayer on the Mount of Olives is very brief, even briefer if we omit verses 43 and 44, which are not found in the earliest manuscripts of his gospel, nor in the other gospels. He does not name the specific place, called *Gethsemane* in Mark (whose text he often follows), but, in keeping with the importance he gives to prayer, Luke has Jesus *twice* tell the disciples to pray that they may not enter into the time of trial or temptation.

Jesus Prays Alone

In Mark, Jesus simply tells the other disciples to sit while he goes off with Peter, James and John to pray. Instead, Luke has Jesus go off alone, and so we are left wondering who would have observed his prayer and his intense sweat (mentioned only by Luke), since all the disciples are asleep (because of grief, Luke alone tells us). Mark mentions Jesus' distress and agitation but Luke does not, nor does he quote Jesus' words about the great grief that he is feeling. Luke

> "PRAY THAT YOU MAY NOT COME INTO THE TIME OF TRIAL."

describes Jesus kneeling to pray, rather than falling to the ground. Finally, he has Jesus return to the sleeping disciples not three times but only once. Being so brief, this account forces us, in Ignatian fashion, to imagine for ourselves what might have happened.

Jesus' Agony

There is a very ancient tradition for accepting the authenticity of verses 43 and 44:

> Then an angel from heaven appeared to him and gave him strength. In his anguish he prayed more earnestly, and his sweat became like great drops of blood falling down on the ground.

They are preserved in most editions of the Bible, though usually with a footnote indicating that some authorities lack them. Here, at least, these two verses provide us with a way of entering more deeply into Jesus' prayer and into his internal struggle to embrace the Father's will. The word *anguish* is often rendered literally as *agony* (*agonia* in Greek, the fear or terror of an athlete before a life-and-death contest or *agon*), so that this scene has traditionally been called "The Agony in the Garden."

Jesus' Dread

Strength from heaven comes to Jesus as an answer to his prayer. And yet his anguish or struggle intensifies, and so does his prayer. Jesus does not sweat blood, rather, his sweat becomes thick and profuse, and the drops of sweat are heavy, *like* drops of blood. Jesus kneels in supplication, instead of throwing himself on the ground (Mt 26:39; Mk 14:35), and he seems to keep his composure, but his internal struggle to face the coming horrendous ordeal calls up dread and triggers all the human instincts to escape. Is this what Jesus is struggling to control? Is this what he means by "my will"? Rather than strain to understand, try simply to be there with him and for him.

"FATHER, IF YOU ARE WILLING, REMOVE THIS CUP FROM ME; YET, NOT MY WILL BUT YOURS BE DONE."

ENTERING INTO CONTEMPLATION

1. CHOOSE WHERE YOU WILL PRAY
   COMPOSE YOURSELF FOR PRAYER

Find a quiet place where you can be alone and uninterrupted for an hour. Take time to be still, to be present to God, and to express both your longing to know the mind and heart of Jesus and your desire to follow him more faithfully in your daily life.

2. IMAGINE THE SCENE

This is a contemplation that is perhaps best done at night or even in the middle of the night. Picture yourself on the Mount of Olives. See the night sky above. Try to imagine the hillside with its olive trees. Below you is the Kidron Valley, and across it are the walls of Jerusalem and the Temple Mount. Rather than place yourself among the sleeping disciples, try simply to be present to Jesus.

3. ASK FOR THIS GRACE

Jesus, draw me into the mystery of your struggle, your agony.

4. LISTEN TO WHAT THE PERSONS SAY

Jesus tells the disciples to "Pray that you may not enter the time of trial." He is encouraging you to pray with him. Recall the other times that you have asked to enter into the mystery of Jesus' prayer, especially the mystery of the Lord's Prayer with its reference to the time of trial. Luke's version does not include the words, "Your will be done . . . ," yet here Jesus says, "Father, . . . not my will but yours be done."

"WHY ARE YOU SLEEPING? GET UP AND PRAY THAT YOU MAY NOT COME INTO THE TIME OF TRIAL."

IN HIS ANGUISH HE PRAYED MORE EARNESTLY, AND HIS SWEAT BECAME LIKE GREAT DROPS OF BLOOD FALLING DOWN ON THE GROUND.

5. ENTER INTO CONVERSATION

You may find yourself drawn to pray with Jesus rather than speak to him. You may find yourself drawn to pray to the Father, as Jesus does. Enter into their communion of hearts and minds. Try to be one with them as they are one.

6. ENTER INTO SILENCE

Let the silence of the night surround you both as you are there with Jesus.

7. CONCLUSION

Thank Jesus for all that you have received in this prayer.

AFTER PRAYING

1. REFLECT ON THE EXPERIENCE

At the end of your contemplation, move to another place and spend a few minutes reviewing your experience of prayer, making note of those things that brought you either consolation or desolation, so that, if you do a repetition or application of the senses, you can return to them again, and enter more deeply into the mystery you are contemplating.

2. QUESTIONS THAT MAY ARISE OUT OF PRAYER

"Not my will but yours be done." Is Jesus' will somehow opposed to the Father's? Is the Father willing Jesus to suffer? Is the Father supporting Jesus on the journey on which he has embarked? Is the coming confrontation with the cross something that both have foreseen and entered into together?

3. SEARCHING THE SCRIPTURES

In the book of Job, at the end of the second chapter (11–13), three of Job's friends go to console and comfort him. "They sat with him on the ground seven days and seven nights, and no one spoke a word to him, for they saw that his suffering was very great." Job, a fictional figure and not a Hebrew, is presented as a just and good man whom God allows Satan to test to see what he is made of.

What to Pray on Next

Having contemplated two of the Lukan gospel passages above, you can do the two repetitions to deepen your experience of prayer, returning to whatever moved you in either consolation or desolation, and then appropriate all that you have been given in an application of senses at the end of the day. Having come to the end of Chapter VI, the sixth day of your retreat, you might look over the material in the next chapter to determine what you will pray on tomorrow.

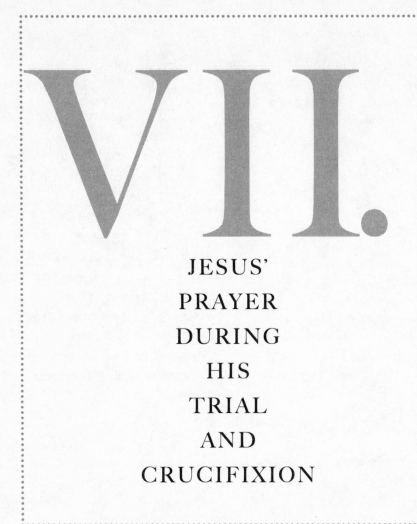

VII.

JESUS' PRAYER DURING HIS TRIAL AND CRUCIFIXION

R ead the preparatory material below and choose two of the following passages for today's prayer.

A. *A Prayerful Glance at Peter:*

   The Mystery of His Love

   Luke 22:54–62

B. *Prayerful Stance Before Herod:*

   The Mystery of His Silence

   Luke 23:6–12

C. *Prayerful Dialogue with Criminals:*

   The Mystery of His Compassion

   Luke 23:33–43

D. *Final Words to the Father:*

   The Mystery of His Humility

   Luke 23:44–49

W hat sustains Jesus throughout his suffering and dying is his prayerful communion with the Father: in spite of everything, he knows that he is not alone.

BACKGROUND

Jesus Is Arrested

Jesus' prayer on the Mount of Olives ends with his abandonment to the Father: "Not my will but yours be done" (22:42). Now the events of the Passion begin to unfold dramatically. There is his betrayal—with a kiss—by Judas, followed by a brief skirmish. At least two of the disciples are armed with swords (22:38). In the clash with the arresting officers, the high priest's servant has his right ear cut off (22:50). This prompts Jesus' final act of healing—an expression of the forgiving love that he preached even for enemies: "But I say to you that listen, Love your enemies, do good to those who hate you, bless those who curse you, pray for those who abuse you" (6:27-28). In Jesus' words to the chief priests, the Temple police, and the elders, Luke has him say, just before his arrest, "But this is your hour, and the power of darkness!" The devil, who tested Jesus in the Judean wilderness and then "departed from him until an opportune time" (4:13), now has his hour—his time of apparent triumph.

Jesus Continues to Pray

After his arrest, Jesus is led to the high priest's house. Peter follows, though at a distance. He is still willing, at this point, to go with Jesus "to prison and to death" (22:33), but he prudently keeps himself well apart from him. The other disciples are not mentioned, and Luke avoids saying that they fled, whereas Mark says that all of them deserted him (14:50). What is going through Jesus' mind during these events? We cannot know—we can only try to imagine. Having been drawn so deeply into Jesus' inner life and into his communion with God in prayer, we can be certain that he is now more conscious than ever of the unbreakable bond between him and the Father. It is possible that, during his Passion, Jesus actually had the commanding presence that Luke gives him in this gospel, but the inner reality of confidence and trust, and the utter conviction of being the Beloved, is surely what Luke is at pains to portray. In the depths of his soul, Jesus is in union with God, and is praying for those who abuse him. If Jesus is praying for his enemies, surely he is praying also for his disciples.

Before You Pray

1. Read the gospel passage slowly and carefully, seeking to understand it more deeply in its totality or in its parts as you wish.

2. Read the section Exploring the Gospel as an aid both to understanding the text and to stimulating your imagination when you pray.

3. Before you begin to pray, read the passage once again.

A. A PRAYERFUL GLANCE AT PETER: THE MYSTERY OF HIS LOVE

LUKE 22:54–62

Then they seized him and led him away, bringing him to the high priest's house. But Peter was following at a distance. When they had kindled a fire in the middle of the courtyard and sat down together, Peter sat among them. Then a servant-girl, seeing him in the firelight, stared at him and said, "This man was with him." But he denied it, saying, "Woman, I do not know him." A little later someone else, on seeing him, said, "You also are one of them." But Peter said, "Man, I am not!" Then about an hour later still another kept insisting, "Surely this man also was with him; for he is a Galilean." But Peter said, "Man, I do not know what you are talking about!" At that moment, while he was still speaking, the cock crowed. The Lord turned and looked at Peter. Then Peter remembered the word of the Lord, how he had said to him, "Before the cock crows today, you will deny me three times." And he went out and wept bitterly. (54–62)

EXPLORING THE GOSPEL

Peter Follows Jesus

The account of Peter's denials reminds us strikingly of Jesus' prayer for Peter. Earlier that same evening at the Passover meal, Jesus had said that Satan would test Peter, and he added, "but I have prayed for you that your own faith may not fail" (22:32). It was this that prompted Peter's declaration that he was ready to follow Jesus anywhere—to prison and even to death. Jesus then prophesied that before cockcrow Peter would three times deny that he knows him. Since Jesus' arrest, Peter has made good his boast, following Jesus, if not to prison then at least to the house of the high priest, where Jesus is to be kept under guard overnight. Peter is among the crowd that sits down in the courtyard, where a fire is kindled in their midst. There a servant-girl recognizes him as one of those who was with Jesus, but Peter denies knowing him. Soon after, a man—probably another servant—accuses Peter of being one of Jesus' followers. Again Peter denies it. Finally, somewhat later, comes a third accusation, and Peter's third denial. Luke has a rooster crow *while Peter is still speaking*, and he is the only evangelist to mention that Jesus turns to look at Peter.

Peter Recalls Jesus' Words

Does Peter remember only the words about betrayal, or does he also remember that Jesus has prayed for him? Does he recall that Jesus prayed that his faith would not fail? Surely his faith has failed now—or has it? Is Peter now totally without faith? Is he bereft of hope? Is he completely lacking in love for Jesus? Perhaps he recalls Jesus' words, "And when once you have turned back. . . ." Does Peter see only the pain in Jesus' eyes, or does he see also Jesus' great love for him, calling him back?

WHEN THEY HAD KINDLED A FIRE IN THE MIDDLE OF THE COURTYARD AND SAT DOWN TOGETHER, PETER SAT AMONG THEM.

AT THAT MOMENT, WHILE HE WAS STILL SPEAKING, THE COCK CROWED. THE LORD TURNED AND LOOKED AT PETER.

ENTERING INTO CONTEMPLATION

1. CHOOSE WHERE YOU WILL PRAY
COMPOSE YOURSELF FOR PRAYER

Find a quiet place where you can be alone and uninterrupted for an hour. Take time to be still, to be present to God, and to express both your longing to know the mind and heart of Jesus and your desire to follow him more faithfully in your daily life.

2. IMAGINE THE SCENE

You can imagine the inner courtyard of the high priest's house, the fire casting its flickering light on the faces of the crowd, and Jesus somewhere in the midst of this group, held or bound, but able to turn and find Peter at the sound of the rooster's crowing. Perhaps Jesus has already seen or heard something of Peter's first two denials. Now, after the third, his eyes meet Peter's. In this one brief glance, Peter is reminded of his boast and of Jesus' prophecy. What does Jesus see in Peter's eyes? What does Peter see in Jesus' eyes? Beyond the inner courtyard is the outer darkness, the darkness of the night into which Peter goes and weeps bitterly. How can he face Jesus? How can he hold his gaze? After the first temptation and failure comes the second and greater temptation: the temptation to despair. You can imagine Peter's anguish and self-loathing. What can possibly save him now from self-destruction? Allow yourself to be drawn back to the look of love in Jesus' eyes. Jesus has no power now but the power of love. This is the only power that saves. Allow Jesus' gaze to meet your own. Try not to turn away. Try simply to dwell in and absorb the boundless love for you that you see in that gaze. Is there any wound that this love cannot heal, or any infidelity that it cannot forgive?

3. ASK FOR THIS GRACE

Jesus, draw me into the mystery of your love—your love for Peter, your love for me.

4. LISTEN TO WHAT THE PERSONS SAY

More important than the words of the three who accuse Peter of being one of Jesus' followers are the words that Peter speaks in denial: "Woman, I do not know him," "Man, I am not!" and "Man, I do not know what you are talking about." Luke omits the words, in Mark 14:71 and Matthew 22:74, that Peter "began to curse and to swear." Jesus needs no words to remind Peter of what he had spoken earlier: "Before the cock crows today, you will deny me three times."

5. ENTER INTO CONVERSATION

When Peter goes out, go out with him. What do you say as you walk and sit together? What do you deeply desire to say to Peter?

6. ENTER INTO SILENCE

Perhaps there is not much you can say or do as Peter weeps and sobs. Try simply to be with him and to comfort him.

7. CONCLUSION

Thank Jesus for all that you have received in this prayer.

AFTER PRAYING

1. REFLECT ON THE EXPERIENCE

At the end of your contemplation, move to another place and spend a few minutes reviewing your experience of prayer, making note of those things that brought you either consolation or

THEN PETER REMEMBERED THE WORD OF THE LORD, HOW HE HAD SAID TO HIM, "BEFORE THE COCK CROWS TODAY, YOU WILL DENY ME THREE TIMES." AND HE WENT OUT AND WEPT BITTERLY.

What to

Pray on Next

Go on to one of the passages in B, C, or D.

desolation, so that, if you do a repetition or application of the senses, you can return to them again, and enter more deeply into the mystery you are contemplating.

2. QUESTIONS THAT MAY ARISE OUT OF PRAYER

In Matthew's gospel (27:3–5) we are told that Judas repented his betrayal of Jesus and then went and hanged himself. Why did Judas take his own life? Why did Peter not do the same?

3. SEARCHING THE SCRIPTURES

You may want to read the Passion narratives in Matthew (chapters 26 and 27) and Mark (chapters 14 and 15). In Exodus 21:32 and Zechariah 11:12–13, thirty shekels of silver is the price of a slave. In Genesis 37:28, Joseph is sold for twenty pieces of silver.

B. PRAYERFUL STANCE BEFORE HEROD: THE MYSTERY OF HIS SILENCE

LUKE 23:6–12

When Pilate heard this, he asked whether the man was a Galilean. And when he learned that he was under Herod's jurisdiction, he sent him off to Herod, who was himself in Jerusalem at that time. When Herod saw Jesus, he was very glad, for he had been wanting to see him for some time. He questioned him at some length, but Jesus gave him no answer. The chief priests and the scribes stood by, vehemently accusing him. Even Herod with his soldiers treated him with contempt and mocked him; then he put an elegant robe on him, and sent him back to Pilate. That same day Herod and Pilate became friends with each other; before this they had been enemies. (23:6–12)

EXPLORING THE GOSPEL

Jesus Is Abused by the Guards

Jesus has become the plaything of his captors. After enduring a night of mockery and abuse (whatever forms this may have taken) at the hands of the temple officers, he is brought before the Council of the Elders, who demand to know whether or not he claims to be the Messiah. Jesus replies, "If I tell you, you will not believe; and if I question you, you will not answer. But from now on the Son of Man will be seated at the right hand of the power of God" (22:67-69). This prompts the council to ask, "Are you, then, the Son of God?", to which Jesus answers, "You say that I am" (22:70). This implied assent seems to be enough to convict Jesus of the offense that they had been hoping for, "so as to hand him over to the jurisdiction and authority of the governor" (20:20). Immediately they go as a group to bring Jesus before Pilate (23:1).

Jesus Is Questioned by Pilate

One of the charges against Jesus is that he claims to be the anointed king or Messiah. When Pilate asks, "Are you the king of the Jews?", Jesus responds with, "You say so." On hearing that Jesus is from Galilee, Pilate has him taken to Herod, who happens to be in Jerusalem. Herod was already aware of Jesus' activity in his territory. Rumors had sprung up concerning Jesus, and word had circulated that Elijah or one of the ancient prophets had appeared—even that John the Baptist had been raised from the dead: "Herod said, 'John I beheaded; but who is this about whom I hear such things?' And he tried to see him" (9:9). Now at last, Herod and Jesus come face to face in a scene that is found only in Luke's gospel.

Jesus Is Questioned by Herod

Herod Antipas, ruler of Galilee, was the son of Herod the Great, King of Judea (mentioned in Luke 1:5). Like his father, he was a puppet of the Romans, a corrupt and immoral man. He was despised by his subjects, and had been denounced by John the Baptist for his illicit marriage. He seems to have considered Jesus to be a sort of wonder-worker "and was hoping to see him perform some sign" (23:8). Now he asks Jesus many questions, but Jesus, who had earlier referred to Herod as "that fox" (13:32), refuses to say anything at all.

HE QUESTIONED HIM AT SOME LENGTH, BUT JESUS GAVE HIM NO ANSWER.

ENTERING INTO CONTEMPLATION

1. CHOOSE WHERE YOU WILL PRAY
    COMPOSE YOURSELF FOR PRAYER

Find a quiet place where you can be alone and uninterrupted for an hour. Take time to be still, to be present to God, and to express both your longing to know the mind and heart of Jesus and your desire to follow him more faithfully in your daily life.

2. IMAGINE THE SCENE

Be present in spirit if not in body. See Jesus as he stands there in silence. It is a humble silence rather than a proud silence. It is not a defiant silence, and yet it is not submissive either. It is a prayerful silence. All those around him are part of his prayer—the chief priests and scribes, the officials and soldiers, Pilate and Herod.

3. ASK FOR THIS GRACE

Jesus, draw me into the mystery of your silence.

4. LISTEN TO WHAT THE PERSONS SAY

The accusations of the chief priests and scribes, the mockery and taunts of Herod's soldiers are not given to us by Luke, but you can easily imagine them. All this apparently has no effect on Jesus. He absorbs it all, and remains silent.

5. ENTER INTO CONVERSATION

Though Jesus is silent and speaks to no one, if you yourself are there as a silent observer, you can will silent words of encouragement.

THE CHIEF PRIESTS AND THE SCRIBES STOOD BY, VEHEMENTLY ACCUSING HIM.

THAT SAME DAY HEROD AND PILATE BECAME FRIENDS WITH EACH OTHER; BEFORE THIS THEY HAD BEEN ENEMIES.

6. ENTER INTO SILENCE

As you ask to be drawn into Jesus' silence, try to see yourself included in his prayer. Try also to see the whole human enterprise included in it as well—all the powerful and all the lowly, all the good and all the evil of all the ages, with all their beauty and all their horror. All of it is caught up in the mercy of God—mercy upon mercy upon mercy. You are part of all this—you, and all your family and all your ancestors. You and they are held in Jesus' wordless communion, in his humility, in his silence.

7. CONCLUSION

Thank Jesus for all that you have received in this prayer.

AFTER PRAYING

1. REFLECT ON THE EXPERIENCE

At the end of your contemplation, move to another place and spend a few minutes reviewing your experience of prayer, making note of those things that brought you either consolation or desolation, so that, if you do a repetition or application of the senses, you can return to them again, and enter more deeply into the mystery you are contemplating.

2. QUESTIONS THAT MAY ARISE OUT OF PRAYER

Is it a result of his prayer that enemies like Herod and Pilate are reconciled? Jesus' prayer is wider and deeper than this. In his prayer, the whole world is being reconciled to God (2 Cor 5:19), a theme that Luke will take up in the Acts of the Apostles as Jesus sends out his apostles to be his witnesses to the ends of the earth (Acts 1:8).

3. SEARCHING THE SCRIPTURES

Chapter 20 of the book of Jeremiah depicts the prophet who was persecuted, beaten by the Temple police, and put in the public stocks for his fearful pronouncements against Jerusalem. In the deuterocanonical book, the Wisdom of Solomon (2:12–22), we find a striking parallel to the Passion of Jesus, in which "the righteous man" is tested with insult and torture and subjected to a shameful death in order to see whether he really is God's child.

What to Pray on Next

If you have contemplated each of the passages above, do two repetitions to deepen the experience and an application of senses. Otherwise go on to one of the passages in C or D.

Before You Pray

1. Read the gospel passage slowly and carefully, seeking to understand it more deeply in its totality or in its parts as you wish.

2. Read the section Exploring the Gospel as an aid both to understanding the text and to stimulating your imagination when you pray.

3. Before you begin to pray, read the passage once again.

C. PRAYERFUL DIALOGUE WITH CRIMINALS: THE MYSTERY OF HIS COMPASSION

LUKE 23:33-43

When they came to the place that is called The Skull, they crucified Jesus there with the criminals, one on his right and one on his left. Then Jesus said, "Father, forgive them; for they do not know what they are doing." And they cast lots to divide his clothing. And the people stood by, watching; but the leaders scoffed at him, saying, "He saved others; let him save himself if he is the Messiah of God, his chosen one!" The soldiers also mocked him, coming up and offering him sour wine, and saying, "If you are the King of the Jews, save yourself!" There was also an inscription over him, "This is the King of the Jews." (33–38)

One of the criminals who were hanged there kept deriding him and saying, "Are you not the Messiah? Save yourself and us!" But the other rebuked him, saying, "Do you not fear God, since you are under the same sentence of condemnation? And we indeed have been condemned justly, for we are getting what we deserved for our deeds, but this man has done nothing wrong." Then he said, "Jesus, remember me when you come into your kingdom." He replied, "Truly I tell you, today you will be with me in Paradise." (39–43)

EXPLORING THE GOSPEL

Jesus Again Before Pilate

Herod sends Jesus back to Pilate, who a second time declares him innocent of any charges deserving death. Perhaps to placate the authorities and the crowd, he says he will have Jesus flogged, and then he will release him. They all cry out instead for the release of Barabbas, a murderer, and for the Crucifixion of Jesus. And, though Pilate protests a third time, he finally gives in to their demands.

Jesus Is Led Away

Luke does not mention that Jesus is actually flogged. He is simply led away to be crucified, and Simon of Cyrene (the major city in the Roman province of Cyrenaica in North Africa), is forced to carry the cross beam. Luke notes that he carries it behind Jesus, recalling Jesus' words, "If any want to become my followers, let them deny themselves and take up their cross daily and follow me" (9:23). On the way, Jesus speaks to some women of Jerusalem who are grieving over him, telling them to weep instead for themselves and for their children, and warning of terrible days to come. Two criminals are led out to be crucified with him.

Jesus Is Crucified

None of the gospels describe how the Crucifixion of Jesus was done, since this would be something that everyone in the Roman Empire was familiar with. There is no need to go into a lot of detail here, except to point out that its purpose was not simply execution but the total humiliation and annihilation of the condemned, as an example and warning to others who might oppose the power of the Roman Empire. The process was meant to be as prolonged, as painful, and as public as possible. No citizen of Rome could be crucified. Crucifixion was reserved for foreign subjects and for slaves.

WHEN THEY CAME TO THE PLACE THAT IS CALLED THE SKULL, THEY CRUCIFIED JESUS THERE WITH THE CRIMINALS, ONE ON HIS RIGHT AND ONE ON HIS LEFT.

AND THE PEOPLE STOOD BY, WATCHING; BUT THE LEADERS SCOFFED AT HIM, SAYING, "HE SAVED OTHERS; LET HIM SAVE HIMSELF IF HE IS THE MESSIAH OF GOD, HIS CHOSEN ONE!"

Jesus Identified with Criminals

When we focus our attention on Jesus alone and forget about the criminals crucified on either side of him, we can miss the essential point, namely, that Jesus is there for them. Though they may have victimized others, they themselves have now become victims. If Jesus had compassion on those who, like lepers, were rejected by society and were thus made to feel that they were rejected also by God, surely he has compassion on these two. Jesus welcomed repentant sinners and ate with them (15:2), and touched lepers in order to heal them (5:13), but here his identification with outcasts is total: he himself is cast out of the Holy City and is crucified with them. As Paul puts it, "For our sake he made him to be sin who knew no sin" (2 Cor 5:21).

The Mystery of Evil

In Jesus' Crucifixion we touch the greatest mystery of all: the mystery of senseless, innocent suffering. Jesus identifies with the two criminals, but he himself is innocent, and so he identifies with all innocent victims as well. Not only is Jesus innocent, he is holy, he is the Son of God (1:35). In Jesus, *God* is cast out and *God* suffers. While the mystery of evil remains and the problem of pain is still unresolved, there can be no question about God's stance: God is not indifferent to human suffering. God is right there in the midst of it, taking it on in the person of Jesus. In Jesus we discover God's full response to human sinfulness, to suffering, and to evil. It is to send the Son as one of us. Jesus enters into the reality of evil—into sin and suffering and death—and takes it upon himself in order to absorb it and transform it: to render it powerless through the power of love.

Jesus' Words of Forgiveness

The words, "Father, forgive them; for they do not know what they are doing" (23:34), are not found in the oldest manuscripts, and many Bibles bracket them for this reason. They do, however, fit the picture of Jesus that Luke has presented: praying at key moments, and pardoning his enemies, as he himself taught his disciples to do (6:27–28). The mystery of this forgiveness is certainly central to the gospel. But the mystery of compassion is also central, and the two go together.

Being with Jesus

In contemplating the Crucifixion, it is difficult to remain passive. We want to be there with Jesus—simply to be present to him in his suffering, as he is present to us in ours. All this horror is in some way foreknown—even in the creation of the universe, and certainly in the creation of free and intelligent human beings who are made in the image and likeness of God. Jesus' birth in the greatest poverty, his life of labor and difficulties, of injuries and affronts, Ignatius tells us, is undertaken "that He may die on the Cross; and all this for me" (*Spiritual Exercises*, paragraph 116). Try especially to focus on compassion—the compassion of God for every living thing (Sir 18:13), the compassion that sends Jesus into the world in the mystery of the Incarnation, the compassion that leads Jesus to follow the path he foresees will bring him to this moment—and then respond to him with your own compassion.

ENTERING INTO CONTEMPLATION

1. CHOOSE WHERE YOU WILL PRAY
   COMPOSE YOURSELF FOR PRAYER

Find a quiet place where you can be alone and uninterrupted for an hour. Take time to be still, to be present to God, and to express both your longing to know the mind and heart of Jesus and your desire to follow him more faithfully in your daily life.

2. IMAGINE THE SCENE

Crucifixion was done outside the city walls, near a well-traveled road or crossroad for maximum exposure. It could be carried out quickly and easily by just two experienced soldiers, who

"FATHER, FORGIVE THEM; FOR THEY DO NOT KNOW WHAT THEY ARE DOING."

stripped the victim completely naked (our crucifixes and other representations usually spare us this fact), and nailed his hands to the cross-beam as he lay on the ground (with your finger and thumb you can find the cavity through which a nail could pass at the base of the palm and through the back of the hand). Then they stood the person on his feet, lifted the beam and fitted it into a projection at the top of an upright post that was permanently set in the place of crucifixion. His dangling feet would almost touch the ground, but next his knees were bent and his feet fastened to the post.

3.   ASK FOR THIS GRACE

Jesus, draw me into the mystery of your compassion.

4.   LISTEN TO WHAT THE PERSONS SAY

The most important role was that of the crowd, who subjected the victim to ridicule, mockery and laughter, while he writhed for hours in agony, struggling to breathe as his muscles went into spasm. This particular crowd certainly did not include the whole people of Jerusalem, the ordinary people, who had welcomed Jesus as king just a few days before (19:38). They were sympathetic to him and hostile towards the chief priests, the religious leaders who were subservient to Rome. The crowd was probably a group organized by the chief priests and the assembly of the elders. Both crucified criminals taunt Jesus in Mark's gospel (15:32), but in Luke's only one of them does, and this one is then rebuked by the other. Like the leaders and the soldiers, but not the people, who stand by watching (23:35), the first criminal taunts Jesus, saying that he should save himself ("and us") if he really is the Messiah. Only in Luke's gospel do we find the second criminal's request, "Jesus, remember me when you come into your kingdom." Jesus' response, "Truly I tell you, today you will be with me in Paradise," acknowledges his kingship and points to a kingdom beyond this world, to which death is the doorway.

THE SOLDIERS ALSO MOCKED HIM, COMING UP AND OFFERING HIM SOUR WINE, AND SAYING,"IF YOU ARE THE KING OF THE JEWS, SAVE YOURSELF."

5. ENTER INTO CONVERSATION

In Luke's gospel, the followers of Jesus stand at a distance, probably kept back from the place of crucifixion by Roman soldiers. Here you can imagine not the apostles but "all his acquaintances, including the women who had followed him from Galilee" (23:49). As you place yourself among the crowd, you might enter briefly into conversation with some of these women.

6. ENTER INTO SILENCE

Confronted by so much human suffering, and in the presence of so much merciless power, you are soon rendered numb and mute.

7. CONCLUSION

Thank Jesus for all that you have received in this prayer.

AFTER PRAYING

1. REFLECT ON THE EXPERIENCE

At the end of your contemplation, move to another place and spend a few minutes reviewing your experience of prayer, making note of those things that brought you either consolation or desolation, so that, if you do a repetition or application of the senses, you can return to them again, and enter more deeply into the mystery you are contemplating.

2. QUESTIONS THAT MAY ARISE OUT OF PRAYER

Why does Jesus not use his power to save the criminals or to save himself? In the taunting words, "If you are the King of the Jews," we are reminded of the testing of Jesus in the wilderness, where twice the tempter begins, "If you are the Son of God . . ." (4:3, 9). Jesus did not use his power then either. During the Passion "the Divinity hides itself," Ignatius tells us in the *Spiritual*

"TRULY I TELL YOU, TODAY YOU WILL BE WITH ME IN PARADISE."

What to Pray on Next

If you have contemplated two of the above passages, do the repetitions and the application of senses. If not, go on to the passage in section D.

Exercises (paragraph 196). Why? How could God ever allow such a thing to happen to Jesus? Is God absent in the Crucifixion? This is the same question that continues to be asked today: "Why was God silent during the Holocaust?" It is the question that is asked of all innocent suffering: "Why? Where is God?"

3. SEARCHING THE SCRIPTURES

How strikingly different from Luke's account of the Crucifixion is the depiction in Mark's gospel, where Jesus' last words are, "My God, my God, why have you forsaken me?" (Mk 15:34). These are the opening words of Psalm 22, which would be worth reading in its entirety to see how the feeling of abandonment is matched with faith in God's power and presence. Though seemingly absent, God is in fact present, commiserating *with* Jesus and suffering *in* Jesus, *with* all those whom the world crucifies. The Song of the Suffering Servant in Isaiah 52:13–53:12 helps to bring out the meaning of Jesus' suffering.

D. FINAL WORDS TO THE FATHER: THE MYSTERY OF HIS HUMILITY

LUKE 23:44–49

Before You Pray

1. Read the gospel passage slowly and carefully, seeking to understand it more deeply in its totality or in its parts as you wish.

2. Read the section Exploring the Gospel as an aid both to understanding the text and to stimulating your imagination when you pray.

3. Before you begin to pray, read the passage once again.

It was now about noon, and darkness had come over the whole land until three in the afternoon, while the sun's light failed; and the curtain of the temple was torn in two. Then Jesus, crying with a loud voice, said, "Father, into your hands I commend my spirit." Having said this, he breathed his last. When the centurion saw what had taken place, he praised God and said, "Certainly this man was innocent." And when all the crowds who had gathered there for this spectacle saw what had taken place, they returned home, beating their breasts. But all his acquaintances, including the women who had followed him from Galilee, stood at a distance, watching these things. (44–49)

EXPLORING THE GOSPEL

Jesus Nears the End

The end is now near. Darkness descends upon the whole land. Luke alone adds that the curtain of the temple is torn in two. In Luke's gospel there is no horrendous cry of abandonment (as in Mark 15:34). There is no attempt to offer Jesus sour wine or vinegar to drink, nor is there any mockery about waiting to see whether Elijah will come to take him down from the cross (Mk 15:36). While neither his mother, nor any of the other women, nor the beloved disciple, is

IT WAS NOW ABOUT NOON, AND DARKNESS HAD COME OVER THE WHOLE LAND UNTIL THREE IN THE AFTERNOON, WHILE THE SUN'S LIGHT FAILED; AND THE CURTAIN OF THE TEMPLE WAS TORN IN TWO.

standing near the cross (as in John 19:25–27), the scene is not quite as bleak as it is in Mark's gospel, where all of the Twelve have fled, leaving Mary Magdalene and many other women looking on from a distance (Mk 15:40). Luke mentions that *all his acquaintances* (does this include the apostles?) together with the women who had followed him from Galilee, stood at a distance watching (23:49).

Jesus Is the Humility of God

What the onlookers see is a human being humiliated and crushed—reduced almost to something less than human. This was their friend, their teacher, their healer, their hoped-for Messiah. What they cannot see is all that lies within this tortured body: the one who "was in the form of God," as Paul puts it, the one who "emptied himself, taking the form of a slave, being born in human likeness. And being found in human form, he humbled himself and became obedient to the point of death—even death on a cross" (Phil 2:6–8). On the cross, Jesus reveals the compassion of God, but, beyond compassion, and more mysterious still, is the humility of God. It is this humility, made manifest in the person of Jesus, that Ignatius invites us to consider and emulate in the "Three Kinds of Humility" described in the *Spiritual Exercises* (paragraphs 165–167).

Jesus Breathes His Last

In Luke's gospel, Jesus' final words from the cross, taken from Psalm 31:5, are a prayer of surrender: "Father, into your hands I commend my spirit." While Mark's portrayal of Jesus' death may seem to be closer to the harsh reality of the Crucifixion (though not even Mark is writing an eye-witness account), Luke's is true to the inner reality that he has been at pains to reveal all through his gospel: Jesus, who lived in continuing communion with God, also dies in communion with God. Jesus, who taught his disciples to call God *Abba, Father,* dies calling God *Father.* Jesus, who modeled confident trust in God during his lifetime, finally shows his disciples how to die, confident of God's fidelity. Jesus, God's beloved Son, who welcomed children, dies confiding his spirit, his entire self, in God's hands, into the Father's welcoming embrace.

Jesus Is Marveled at and Mourned

When Jesus finally dies surrendering himself to God, the one who sees him breathe his last and who praises God, exclaiming that he was innocent, is the Roman officer in charge of the soldiers—a Gentile and a pagan. Luke is alone in adding that the crowds, who had been silently observing the Crucifixion, go home beating their breasts (23:48)—a gesture of grief and mourning rather than of guilt.

ENTERING INTO CONTEMPLATION

1. CHOOSE WHERE YOU WILL PRAY
   COMPOSE YOURSELF FOR PRAYER

Find a quiet place where you can be alone and uninterrupted for an hour. Take time to be still, to be present to God, and to express both your longing to know the mind and heart of Jesus and your desire to follow him more faithfully in your daily life.

2. IMAGINE THE SCENE

Place yourself among Jesus' friends and disciples, among the Galilean women and his acquaintances.

3. ASK FOR THIS GRACE

Jesus, draw me into the mystery of your humility and death on the cross.

4. LISTEN TO WHAT THE PERSONS SAY

Listen to Jesus' loud cry and his final words. Hear the Roman centurion praise God and declare Jesus innocent. Imagine the response of the friends of Jesus as they see him die.

AND WHEN ALL THE CROWDS WHO HAD GATHERED THERE FOR THIS SPECTACLE SAW WHAT HAD TAKEN PLACE, THEY RETURNED HOME, BEATING THEIR BREASTS.

5. ENTER INTO CONVERSATION

Speak to Jesus as he dies, if you are moved to speak to him, or express your feelings to one of his friends.

6. ENTER INTO SILENCE

Enter into the awful silence that falls over the crowd. Contemplate all that happens, taking it into your heart. Watch as the people around you slowly depart, grieving. Remain there in still-ness as Jesus hangs on the cross in death.

7. CONCLUSION

Thank Jesus for all that you have received in this prayer.

AFTER PRAYING

1. REFLECT ON THE EXPERIENCE

At the end of your contemplation, move to another place and spend a few minutes reviewing your experience of prayer, making note of those things that brought you either consolation or desolation, so that, if you do a repetition or application of the senses, you can return to them again, and enter more deeply into the mystery you are contemplating.

2. QUESTIONS THAT MAY ARISE OUT OF PRAYER

There can be no question that Jesus really dies on the cross. The grief of his friends and fol-lowers, who witnessed his death, is attested to in all four gospels. Which accounts give us the most accurate picture? Remembering that the gospels are attempts to preserve something of the proclamation of the apostles in the decades after Jesus' death and resurrection, we can say that each of the gospels seeks to bring out the meaning of the events as passed on in this preaching. As a Gentile, Luke is not an authority on Jewish ritual, and as someone from outside of Palestine,

"FATHER, INTO YOUR HANDS I COMMEND MY SPIRIT."

he is not entirely familiar with its language, topography, and buildings. But, as he says in the introduction to his gospel, he has investigated everything carefully, and has tried to write an orderly account for his readers, so that they may know the truth about these things (1:1–4).

3. SEARCHING THE SCRIPTURES

You may want to read through the whole of Psalm 31, having heard part of it on Jesus' lips as he dies. David's lament in 2 Samuel 1:19–27 is a very personal expression of grief for Saul and especially for Jonathan, his friend, and could be applied in part to the death of Jesus, the Son of David. The book of Lamentations, ascribed to Jeremiah, is a fitting expression of grief for Jesus as well as for the destruction of Jerusalem: "How lonely sits the city that was once full of people!" (1:1).

What to Pray on Next

In coming to the end of chapter VII, you have come to the end of the seventh day of your retreat. Having contemplated two of the scripture passages, do two repetitions to deepen the experience of following Jesus right to the cross. All that is implicit in the cost of discipleship becomes clear and explicit in the final stages of this following. Try to appropriate this in the application of senses.

VIII.

JESUS RISEN AND ASCENDED IN PRAYER

Read the preparatory material below and choose two of the following passages for today's prayer.

A. Opening the Scriptures:

The Mystery of His Risen Life

Luke 24:13–27

B. Breaking the Bread:

The Mystery of His Presence

Luke 24:28–35

C. Comforting His Friends:

The Mystery of His Consolation

Luke 24:36–49

D. Blessing the Disciples:

The Mystery of His Glory

Luke 24:50–53

Jesus, who died and who was raised to the fullness of life with the Father in the Spirit, now intercedes for us in an unceasing, loving dialogue.

BACKGROUND

Jesus Is Placed in the Tomb

The entombment of Jesus by Joseph of Arimathea, a sympathetic member of the council, who procures permission from Pilate to remove Jesus' body from the cross, brings the story of the Passion to its conclusion, as the Galilean women return to their homes to prepare burial spices and ointments (23:50–56).

The Tomb Is Found Empty

After resting on the Sabbath, the women—Mary Magdalene, Joanna, Mary the mother of James, and two others (24:10)—revisit the tomb at dawn on the first day of the week, only to find the stone that had sealed the tomb is rolled aside. The body of Jesus is missing. Suddenly, two men in dazzling clothes appear and tell them that Jesus is risen, and remind them that he had foretold this. The women go back and report to the Eleven, who do not believe them. Peter runs to the tomb to verify their story and, peering into the empty tomb, he sees the linen cloths that had covered Jesus' body. He returns home amazed (24:1–12).

Jesus Has Passed Through Death to New Life

There is no account in any of the gospels of Jesus' resurrection itself. What we have are accounts of the empty tomb and of *post-resurrection appearances*. The resurrection is not something that can be verified by empirical investigation.

Its verification lies in the changed lives of those who saw the risen Jesus after his death on the cross. What they experienced was not a resuscitated Jesus—not someone who came out of the tomb the way Lazarus did (Jn 11:44), not someone who would go back to living in a house, like Lazarus (Jn 12:1–2), and not someone who would have to die again, like Lazarus (Jn 12:10). What they experienced was a Jesus who had passed through death to enter another kind of life—to "enter into His glory" (Lk 24:26). Jesus' words to one of the criminals crucified with him would seem to reveal when this occurred, that is, on the very day of his death: "Truly I tell you, today you will be with me in Paradise" (23:43).

Jesus' Post-Resurrection Appearances

The absence of his body from the tomb is the first indication that this body is also part of the new life that Jesus has entered. The post-resurrection appearances are what make this clear. Jesus appears in the flesh, and he bodily manifests himself to his disciples for brief periods of time, and then vanishes. He is not a ghostly phantom or disembodied spirit: "Touch me and see; for a ghost does not have flesh and bones as you see that I have" (24:39). And yet, for some reason, his disciples do not at first recognize him. This is what we find in Luke's story of the two disciples on the road to Emmaus, expanding just two verses in Mark's gospel (16:12–13), which say that Jesus "appeared in another form to two of them, as they were walking into the country."

1. Read the gospel passage slowly and carefully, seeking to understand it more deeply in its totality or in its parts as you wish.

2. Read the section Exploring the Gospel as an aid both to understanding the text and to stimulating your imagination when you pray.

3. Before you begin to pray, read the passage once again.

A. OPENING THE SCRIPTURES: THE MYSTERY OF HIS RISEN LIFE

LUKE 24:13–27

Now on that same day two of them were going to a village called Emmaus, about seven miles from Jerusalem, and talking with each other about all these things that had happened. While they were talking and discussing, Jesus himself came near and went with them, but their eyes were kept from recognizing him. And he said to them, "What are you discussing with each other while you walk along?" They stood still, looking sad. Then one of them, whose name was Cleopas, answered him, "Are you the only stranger in Jerusalem who does not know the things that have taken place there in these days?" He asked them, "What things?" They replied, "The things about Jesus of Nazareth, who was a prophet mighty in deed and word before God and all the people, and how our chief priests and leaders handed him over to be condemned to death and crucified him. But we had hoped that he was the one to redeem Israel. Yes, and besides all this, it is now the third day since these things took place. Moreover, some women of our group astounded us. They were at the tomb early this morning, and when they did not find his body there, they came back and told us that they had seen a vision of angels who said that he was alive. Some of those who were with us went to the tomb and found it just as the women had said; but they did not see him." Then he said to them, "Oh, how foolish you are, and slow of heart to believe all that the prophets have declared! Was it not necessary that the Messiah should suffer these things and then enter into his glory?" Then beginning with Moses and all the prophets, he interpreted to them the things about himself in all the scriptures. (24:13–27)

EXPLORING THE GOSPEL

Two Disciples on the Road

If you want to contemplate the story of the disciples on the road to Emmaus in two prayer periods, you could focus first on what happens before they arrive at their destination. The account begins "on that same day," that is, on the first day of the week. The two set out on foot from Jerusalem for a town not far away, less than two hours' journey. If they were among the acquaintances of Jesus who observed his crucifixion, even from a distance, the effect on them would have been traumatic. Their hearts are broken, their hopes are shattered. They are discussing together all that had recently happened in Jerusalem, when Jesus himself joins them and asks what they are talking about. We're told that "their eyes were kept from recognizing him" (24:16). It is difficult to know what this could mean, but it does not mean that Jesus was so transformed or transfigured in resurrection that he was no longer recognizable. If this were the case, the other disciples would not be terrified when he appears again later (24:37), for they would not recognize him either. The attention is not on Jesus' appearance, but on the two disciples, whose eyes were "held" or (in the archaic wording of the Authorized or King James Version) "holden so that they should not know Him" (24:16).

Two Disciples in Desolation

Perhaps their inability to recognize Jesus should be attributed to their state of dejection and sadness (24:17) or, to use an Ignatian term, their state of *spiritual desolation*. It has begun with their loss of hope, ". . . we had hoped that he was the one to redeem Israel" (24:21), and left them without faith as well (Jesus, it seems, was *not* the one they had believed him to be). This fits with

WHILE THEY WERE TALKING AND DISCUSSING, JESUS HMSELF CAME NEAR AND WENT WITH THEM, BUT THEIR EYES WERE KEPT FROM RECOGNIZING HIM.

the definition and the dynamic of spiritual desolation as found in the *Spiritual Exercises* (paragraphs 316–317), and it fits also with the way that the moment of recognition, when it finally occurs at the breaking of the bread, comes not simply through physical seeing but through the eyes of faith: "Then their eyes were opened, and they recognized him" (24:31).

Two Disciples in Conversation with Jesus

Our focus here, though, is on the conversation they have with Jesus as they walk together. Because Jesus is not recognized, he is able to lead them on with his questions. There is unconscious irony in their response, when they ask in turn whether Jesus is "the only stranger in Jerusalem who does not know the things that have taken place there in these days." Jesus is hardly a stranger, and of all those in Jerusalem he is the only one who *really knows*—who has *experienced*—all that happened. With further questioning, Jesus is able to get them to tell him about these events, including those of that very morning, when the empty tomb was discovered. The disciples' lack of faith is further disclosed when they mention the vision of angels at the tomb and the message to the women, saying that Jesus is alive. They add, however, that they did not see *him*. They are clearly among those to whom this seemed "an idle tale" (24:11).

Jesus Explains the Scriptures

Luke does not tell us exactly what passages of scripture Jesus interpreted or explained to these disciples, but he makes it clear that Jesus went through "all the scriptures" (24:27), touching on those passages that pertain to him. Instead of trying to discover what these might be by searching through your bible, try instead to place yourself with Jesus as one of these disciples.

"ARE YOU THE ONLY STRANGER IN JERUSALEM WHO DOES NOT KNOW THE THINGS THAT HAVE TAKEN PLACE THERE IN THESE DAYS?"

ENTERING INTO CONTEMPLATION

1. CHOOSE WHERE YOU WILL PRAY
COMPOSE YOURSELF FOR PRAYER

Find a quiet place where you can be alone and uninterrupted for an hour. Take time to be still, to be present to God, and to express both your longing to know the mind and heart of Jesus and your desire to follow him more faithfully in your daily life.

2. IMAGINE THE SCENE

If you have ever experienced deep spiritual desolation, with all its accompanying loss of hope and faith, recall how that felt, and try to imagine the effect of hearing Jesus expound the scriptures to you. The disciples, having been "slow of heart to believe" (24:25), will later say that their hearts were burning within them (24:32). Try to imagine your own hope and faith being kindled anew within you as you listen to Jesus.

3. ASK FOR THIS GRACE

Jesus, draw me into the mystery of your risen life.

4. LISTEN TO WHAT THE PERSONS SAY

There is a power in the word of God, a power that is able to raise you from a state of desolation to one of consolation. When you put the words of scripture on the risen Christ's lips and allow him in imagination to recite them to your wounded and broken heart, amazing things can happen. It is in woundedness and brokenness that your heart is opened to receive the word:

> The Lord is near to the brokenhearted,
>
> and saves the crushed in spirit. (Ps 34:18)

"OH, HOW FOOLISH YOU ARE, AND SLOW OF HEART TO BELIEVE ALL THAT THE PROPHETS HAVE DECLARED!"

What words of scripture have brought you hope and healing in the past? Imagine Jesus speaking them to you now. Let their power penetrate your heart and soul.

5. ENTER INTO CONVERSATION

It is not a matter of pretending that, like these two disciples, you do not recognize Jesus, but rather of simply telling him what is in your heart at this moment. Perhaps you recall and share some of the times when, in the past, you could not recognize how he was there at work in your life.

6. ENTER INTO SILENCE

There are moments of what Ignatius calls confusion (*Spiritual Exercises*, paragraph 48), moments when we are left speechless at the realization of our own blindness or obtuseness, moments when we find ourselves reduced to silence. What are you feeling as you still your words and thoughts?

7. CONCLUSION

Thank Jesus for all that you have received in this prayer.

AFTER PRAYING

1. REFLECT ON THE EXPERIENCE

At the end of your contemplation, move to another place and spend a few minutes reviewing your experience of prayer, making note of those things that brought you either consolation or desolation, so that, if you do a repetition or application of the senses, you can return to them again, and enter more deeply into the mystery you are contemplating.

"BUT WE HAD HOPED THAT HE WAS THE ONE TO REDEEM ISRAEL."

2. QUESTIONS THAT MAY ARISE IN PRAYER

"Was it not necessary that the Messiah should suffer these things and then enter into his glory?" Could God not have accomplished our salvation in some other way and without all this suffering? Did Jesus really have to suffer and die? Is it possible that love could see no better way to reveal itself to us than to suffer with us this way?

3. SEARCHING THE SCRIPTURES

In the book of Job (40:3–5 and 42:1–6), we see Job's response to God when, after much suffering, he finally begins to acknowledge his ignorance and to understand something of God's purposes, and is reduced to silence.

What to Pray on Next

Go on to one of the passages in B, C, or D.

Before You Pray

1. Read the gospel passage slowly and carefully, seeking to understand it more deeply in its totality or in its parts as you wish.

2. Read the section Exploring the Gospel as an aid both to understanding the text and to stimulating your imagination when you pray.

3. Before you begin to pray, read the passage once again.

B. BREAKING THE BREAD: THE MYSTERY OF HIS PRESENCE

LUKE 24:28–35

As they came near the village to which they were going, he walked ahead as if he were going on. But they urged him strongly, saying, "Stay with us, because it is almost evening and the day is now nearly over." So he went in to stay with them. When he was at the table with them, he took bread, blessed and broke it, and gave it to them. Then their eyes were opened, and they recognized him; and he vanished from their sight. They said to each other, "Were not our hearts burning within us while he was talking to us on the road, while he was opening the scriptures to us?" That same hour they got up and returned to Jerusalem; and they found the eleven and their companions gathered together. They were saying, "The Lord has risen indeed, and he has appeared to Simon!" Then they told what had happened on the road, and how he had been made known to them in the breaking of the bread. (28–35)

EXPLORING THE GOSPEL

The Shape of Liturgy

The account of Jesus and the disciples on the road to Emmaus (which takes place on the first day of the week) has the shape of a Sunday worship, at least as it has come to be structured: the scriptures are broken open and explained. The breaking of the bread then takes place. The phrase "the breaking of the bread" (24:35) came to denote the celebration of the Eucharist in Luke's second book (Acts 2:42), and it probably has this meaning here as well. It is possible to read the story in that context, seeing it as a kind of liturgical prayer experience.

Communion

But Jesus' prayer, as Luke has depicted it in this gospel, is nothing less than his continuing communion with the Father. With Jesus' entrance into his glory, this communion is now complete, and so the post-resurrection appearances here can be seen as taking place within the context of this communion, drawing the disciples deeper and deeper into it. From the glory of this "fullness" of communion, Jesus appears, not to those who rejected him but to his followers. What the risen Jesus leaves with the community of his disciples, with "those who from the beginning were eye witnesses and servants of the word" (1:2) is his mysterious presence, his sacramental presence, in the action of the Eucharist. The Eucharist is not just a liturgical prayer experience. It is our continued sharing in Jesus' heavenly communion in the Trinity.

Real Presence

It is his unseen presence that needs to be recognized by all who follow Jesus. The risen Lord walks unrecognized with his disciples. Is he not still with them after he vanishes? Is that not the point of this experience? The word of God in the scriptures points us to a presence that is unseen, and the Eucharist makes that presence tangible.

WHEN HE WAS AT THE TABLE WITH THEM, HE TOOK BREAD, BLESSED AND BROKE IT, AND GAVE IT TO THEM.

THEN THEIR EYES
WERE OPENED,
AND THEY RECOGNIZED
HIM. . . .

Bread Blessed and Broken

The disciples arrive at the village, where they have a house, and they invite Jesus to join them for a simple meal. Though Jesus is the guest, he assumes the role of head of the household as he takes the bread, says the blessing over it, breaks it and gives it to the others. The words recall those used in the multiplication of the loaves and fishes (9:16), though the phrase "he looked up to heaven" is omitted. No doubt there were many meals with the disciples (apart from the Last Supper) at which Jesus presided in this way, and it may be the surprise of finding themselves again in this relation of disciples to master that opens their eyes. But if so, then surely they were also in relation to Jesus this way as he taught them on the road and opened the scriptures to them: their hearts burning within them should have told them this, but still they did not recognize him.

Eucharist

Luke seems to imply, by the use of the phrase "the breaking of the bread," that this was not just an ordinary meal but that it was a Eucharist, and that this is what opened their eyes to recognize Jesus as present, as risen, and as the Messiah about whom he had spoken with them on the road. But as soon as he is recognized, he vanishes. It is not just to share the Eucharist with them, however, that Jesus appears to these two disciples, but to bring them to this moment of fuller recognition: that Jesus has actually joined them, has walked with them, has talked with them, has opened the scriptures to them and broken the bread with them. He is alive, and he is with them still!

ENTERING INTO CONTEMPLATION

1. CHOOSE WHERE YOU WILL PRAY
   COMPOSE YOURSELF FOR PRAYER

Find a quiet place where you can be alone and uninterrupted for an hour. Take time to be still, to be present to God, and to express both your longing to know the mind and heart of Jesus and your desire to follow him more faithfully in your daily life.

2. IMAGINE THE SCENE

Try once again to see yourself as one of these disciples. Imagine the village of Emmaus and the small stone house that they invite Jesus to enter with them. Sit at the table with Jesus.

3. ASK FOR THIS GRACE

Jesus, draw me into the mystery of your presence.

4. LISTEN TO WHAT THE PERSONS SAY

Listen especially to what Jesus says as he unexpectedly assumes the role of host and pronounces the words of blessing over the bread: "Blessed are You, O Lord our God. . . ."

5. ENTER INTO CONVERSATION

What is it like to have your eyes opened in faith—in recognition of the risen Jesus? Instead of being crestfallen at his vanishing, join in the excitement of sharing your feelings with each other. Feel your own hope come alive and your faith increase.

6. ENTER INTO SILENCE

The world remains unchanged, but do you look at it now through new eyes? What new feelings do you experience as you gaze on everything around you? Do words fail you? Try simply to

"WERE NOT OUR HEARTS BURNING WITHIN US WHILE HE WAS TALKING TO US ON THE ROAD, WHILE HE WAS OPENING THE SCRIPTURES TO US?"

What to Pray on Next

If you have contemplated both the passages above, go on to the repetitions and the application of senses. Otherwise pray over one of the passages in section C or D.

savor what you have just experienced. Do you feel impelled eventually, like Mary after the annunciation, to share this good news with others?

7. CONCLUSION

Thank Jesus for all that you have received in this prayer.

AFTER PRAYING

1. REFLECT ON THE EXPERIENCE

At the end of your contemplation, move to another place and spend a few minutes reviewing your experience of prayer, making note of those things that brought you either consolation or desolation, so that, if you do a repetition or application of the senses, you can return to them again, and enter more deeply into the mystery you are contemplating.

2. QUESTIONS THAT MAY ARISE IN PRAYER

Why should Jesus vanish so abruptly? If he was willing to converse at such length with the two disciples on the way to Emmaus, why would he not remain with them after they recognize him, to answer some of the many questions they surely would have had? Is there a wisdom in leaving them to search for answers on their own?

3. SEARCHING THE SCRIPTURES

Matthew's gospel ends with one brief account of the risen Jesus appearing to the Eleven in Galilee (28:16–20). There he sends them to make disciples of all nations and to baptize in the name of the Trinity. His final words are, "I am with you always, to the end of the age." Mark's gospel has two or three possible endings. Mark 16:9–20 includes the sending of the Eleven and the signs that believers will perform.

C. COMFORTING HIS FRIENDS: THE MYSTERY OF HIS CONSOLATION

LUKE 24:36-49

While they were talking about this, Jesus himself stood among them and said to them, "Peace be with you." They were startled and terrified, and thought that they were seeing a ghost. He said to them, "Why are you frightened, and why do doubts arise in your hearts? Look at my hands and my feet; see that it is I myself. Touch me and see, for a ghost does not have flesh and bones as you see that I have." And when he had said this, he showed them his hands and his feet. While in their joy they were disbelieving and still wondering, he said to them, "Have you anything here to eat?" They gave him a piece of broiled fish, and he took it and ate in their presence. (36–43)

Then he said to them, "These are my words that I spoke to you while I was still with you—that everything written about me in the law of Moses, the prophets, and the psalms must be fulfilled. Then he opened their minds to understand the scriptures, and he said to them, "Thus it is written, that the Messiah is to suffer and to rise from the dead on the third day, and that repentance and forgiveness of sins is to be proclaimed in his name to all nations, beginning from Jerusalem. You are witnesses of these things. And see, I am sending upon you what my Father promised; so stay here in the city until you have been clothed with power from on high." (44–49)

EXPLORING THE GOSPEL

Rejoice in the Risen Jesus

The joy of the risen Jesus is something Ignatius calls our attention to in the *Spiritual Exercises*, telling us to "ask for the grace to rejoice and be glad intensely at so great glory and joy of Christ our Lord" (paragraph 221). Jesus has come into the world, has lived his very ordinary life, has taken on his prophetic mission, has brought hope to the despairing, has confronted the rich, has challenged the powerful, has died with the outcast, and has now revealed a glimpse of a new reality to those closest to him. He has done all this with infinite humility and out of boundless love—love for the Father who sent him and love for all those to whom he was sent. We should try to appreciate how, having returned with his human nature to the divine source from which he came, Jesus must now be rejoicing in the Holy Spirit as he once did earlier with his disciples after watching "Satan fall from heaven like a flash of lightning" (10:17–24).

Be Consoled by the Risen Jesus

Ignatius also suggests that we consider the "office" or ministry of consoling that the risen Jesus now assumes, saying that we can compare it with how friends normally console one another (*Spiritual Exercises,* paragraph 224). Jesus' disciples and friends have suffered through his ordeal with him, and so it is to them that he appears and it is they whom he desires to console. "I call it consolation when some interior movement in the soul is caused, through which the soul comes to be inflamed with love of its Creator and Lord . . ." (*Spiritual Exercises*, paragraph 316). Spiritual consolation, for Ignatius, is the spilling over of God's love in our interior being. Jesus' opening of the scriptures to the disciples on the road to Emmaus inflames their hearts with love,

WHILE THEY WERE TALKING ABOUT THIS, JESUS HIMSELF STOOD AMONG THEM AND SAID TO THEM, "PEACE BE WITH YOU."

opening of the scriptures to the disciples on the road to Emmaus inflames their hearts with love, and this love fills them with a joy that they are burning to share with the rest of their friends. And so they hurry back to Jerusalem, only to find that Jesus has been there ahead of them and has been seen by Simon Peter.

Believe in the Risen Jesus

The disciples gathered in Jerusalem are surprised by yet another appearance of Jesus—terrified even, and doubting and unbelieving. Jesus shows them the marks of his Crucifixion by which they can verify that he is truly the one they had seen die on the cross. "In their joy they were disbelieving and still wondering," Luke says, the emphasis being on their joy: they are beside themselves with joy—this all seems too good to be true, as we might express it in other words. Jesus even eats something to demonstrate his earthly reality. And once again he goes through the scriptures, recalling passages that deal with his death and resurrection. This time he mentions the psalms, traditionally attributed to David, many of which (the "Christological Psalms") Christians now put on the lips of Jesus, the Son of David.

ENTERING INTO CONTEMPLATION

1. CHOOSE WHERE YOU WILL PRAY
   COMPOSE YOURSELF FOR PRAYER

Find a quiet place where you can be alone and uninterrupted for an hour. Take time to be still, to be present to God, and to express both your longing to know the mind and heart of Jesus and your desire to follow him more faithfully in your daily life.

2. IMAGINE THE SCENE

As you place yourself among the many disciples and friends of Jesus in this room, try to feel their joy at seeing Jesus alive. Try also to feel something of *his* joy—the joy he desires to share

"TOUCH ME AND SEE, FOR A GHOST DOES NOT HAVE FLESH AND BONES AS YOU SEE THAT I HAVE." AND WHEN HE HAD SAID THIS, HE SHOWED THEM HIS HANDS AND HIS FEET.

with them as he embraces them and reassures them of the reality of his presence—and the truth of his deepest self as revealed in the scriptures.

3. ASK FOR THIS GRACE

Jesus, draw me into the mystery of your consolation.

4. LISTEN TO WHAT THE PERSONS SAY

Jesus speaks many words during this appearance, beginning with *Shalom*, "Peace be with you" (24:36). Which of his many words hold the most meaning for you? Which stir the deepest feeling?

5. ENTER INTO CONVERSATION

Feel your own consolation swell, as your hope, your faith in Jesus, and your love for him grow stronger. How can you put all this (or any of it) into words? Can you try?

6. ENTER INTO SILENCE

Though words are important, perhaps a time will come when you can express your love in deeds, which count for more than words (*Spiritual Exercises*, paragraph 230).

7. CONCLUSION

Thank Jesus for all that you have received in this prayer.

AFTER PRAYING

1. REFLECT ON THE EXPERIENCE

At the end of your contemplation, move to another place and spend a few minutes reviewing your experience of prayer, making note of those things that brought you either consolation or

THEN HE OPENED THEIR MINDS TO UNDERSTAND THE SCRIPTURES. . . .

desolation, so that, if you do a repetition or application of the senses, you can return to them again, and enter more deeply into the mystery you are contemplating.

2. QUESTIONS THAT MAY ARISE IN PRAYER

Is it at all possible that, in this appearing of the risen Jesus, the disciples are seeing a ghost, a phantom, a disembodied spirit? Jesus shows them his hands and his feet, no doubt to display his wounds, but why would his risen and glorified body still have wounds or scars? Jesus asks for something to eat, again to show that he is not a ghost, but what need would he now have for earthly food?

3. SEARCHING THE SCRIPTURES

The appearance of the risen Jesus to the disciples in John 20:19–20 seems to echo the appearance in Luke 24:36–43. In chapter 21 of John's gospel, there is the account of Jesus appearing to the disciples by the Sea of Tiberias (the Sea or Lake of Galilee). When the disciples come ashore, they find bread and a charcoal fire with fish cooking on it (Jn 21:9). Jesus invites them to have breakfast, which would imply that he also eats with them. There are still lingering questions about Jesus, but "none of the disciples dared to ask him 'Who are you?' because they knew it was the Lord" (Jn 21:12).

What to Pray on Next

If you have contemplated two of the above passages, do the repetitions and the application of senses. If not, go on to the passage in D.

212

Before You Pray

1. Read the gospel passage slowly and carefully, seeking to understand it more deeply in its totality or in its parts as you wish.

2. Read the section Exploring the Gospel as an aid both to understanding the text and to stimulating your imagination when you pray.

3. Before you begin to pray, read the passage once again.

D. BLESSING THE DISCIPLES: THE MYSTERY OF HIS GLORY

LUKE 24:50–53

Then he led them out as far as Bethany, and, lifting up his hands, he blessed them. While he was blessing them, he withdrew from them and was carried up into heaven. And they worshipped him, and returned to Jerusalem with great joy; and they were continually in the temple blessing God. (50–53)

EXPLORING THE GOSPEL

The Risen Jesus Lives Elsewhere

In his second volume, the Acts of the Apostles, Luke says of Jesus, "After his suffering he presented himself alive to them by many convincing proofs, appearing to them during forty days and speaking about the kingdom of God" (Acts 1:3). The next verse begins, "While *staying* with them" (1:4), which implies that Jesus remained on earth during these forty days, but the phrase could also be translated, "While *eating* with them" or "being assembled together with them" (King James or Authorized Version). In Luke's gospel, however, Jesus makes only three appearances, all on "the first day of the week," and then, that same evening, he leads them out of Jerusalem to Bethany and is carried up into heaven (24:51). However long these appearances may have gone on (over the course of one day or over forty days), Luke's gospel helps us to see that the risen Jesus *did not remain on earth* for a period of time *before* he joined the Father in heaven. The risen Jesus *is* in heaven, but, no longer limited by time and space, he is able also to be with his disciples on earth.

The Witness of Changed Lives

The impact of these post-resurrection appearances by Jesus on the lives of his disciples is enough to demonstrate the authenticity of Jesus' resurrection. From being desolate and without hope after Jesus' Crucifixion, they are soon moved to preach the reality of his resurrection, and even to lay down their lives out of love for him and in emulation of him, as Luke will show in the Acts of the Apostles. The commission to witness to him—to proclaim his death and resurrection, and to proclaim repentance and forgiveness of sins in his name—is given by Jesus to the Eleven "and their companions" (24:33), together with the promise of power from on high (24:46–49). In the meantime, they are to remain in Jerusalem. Then, Jesus withdraws from them.

Jesus' Entrance Into Glory

From all that Luke has given us in his gospel, it would seem that Jesus' ascension, his being "carried up into heaven," is not the beginning of his entrance into glory, but rather the end of his appearances *after* that entrance into glory—an entrance that was accomplished with the resurrection. This is the meaning of his words to the disciples on the road to Emmaus on resurrection day: "Was it not necessary that the Messiah should suffer these things and then enter into his glory?" (24:26). Borne out by his vanishing at the breaking of the bread (24:31), he returns to his heavenly dwelling place. This time, however, at the ascension, Jesus does not vanish but withdraws (literally translated, he is *separated* or *parted*) from the disciples in the act of blessing them.

THEN HE LED THEM OUT AS FAR AS BETHANY, AND LIFTING UP HIS HANDS, HE BLESSED THEM.

> **"T**HUS IT IS
> WRITTEN, THAT
> THE MESSIAH IS TO
> SUFFER AND TO RISE
> FROM THE DEAD ON THE
> THIRD DAY, AND THAT
> REPENTANCE AND
> FORGIVENESS OF SINS IS
> TO BE PROCLAIMED IN
> HIS NAME TO ALL
> NATIONS, BEGINNING
> FROM JERUSALEM."

ENTERING INTO CONTEMPLATION

1. CHOOSE WHERE YOU WILL PRAY
COMPOSE YOURSELF FOR PRAYER

Find a quiet place where you can be alone and uninterrupted for an hour. Take time to be still, to be present to God, and to express both your longing to know the mind and heart of Jesus and your desire to follow him more faithfully in your daily life.

2. IMAGINE THE SCENE

At the end of the day, that first day of the week, Jesus leads his disciples to the town of Bethany. Picture the darkened scene, the night sky. Place yourself among the disciples whom Jesus blesses. His word of blessing is expressed also with a gesture. However you imagine it, it is a form of prayer, coming from the heart of his communion with the Father, and imparting the Trinity's love and protection. The disciples bow down in worship of Jesus in this moment.

3. ASK FOR THIS GRACE

Jesus, draw me into the mystery of your glory.

4. LISTEN TO WHAT THE PERSONS SAY

Go back to the verses at the end of the passage in section C (Lk 24:46–49), where Jesus tells the apostles that they are to proclaim repentance and forgiveness of sins in his name to all the nations, and that they are to be witness of his suffering, death, and resurrection. Listen to the promise that they will be clothed with power from on high. You too have been graced and gifted with the Holy Spirit—your living link with Jesus.

5. ENTER INTO CONVERSATION

There doesn't seem to be much place for conversation with Jesus in this scene, though you may want to talk with some of the others after Jesus withdraws from sight.

6. ENTER INTO SILENCE

You are not watching a great leap into space (though that seems to be the image behind the tradition that Jesus left the imprint of his foot on the stone now covered by the Dome of the Ascension, outside Jerusalem). The text simply says that Jesus *withdrew*. You are filled with the awareness that he will not be appearing again in his risen body. Something is coming to an end, and something new is about to begin. You bow down in worship with the others.

7. CONCLUSION

Thank Jesus for all that you have received in this prayer.

AFTER PRAYING

1. REFLECT ON THE EXPERIENCE

At the end of your contemplation, move to another place and spend a few minutes reviewing your experience of prayer, making note of those things that brought you either consolation or desolation, so that, if you do a repetition or application of the senses, you can return to them again, and enter more deeply into the mystery you are contemplating.

2. QUESTIONS THAT MAY ARISE IN PRAYER

Was it real? Or was it all a dream? The great joy with which the apostles return to Jerusalem is a gift of spiritual consolation, confirming the reality of what they have experienced. That joy and that reality will sustain them through their remaining days and years as they begin anew their following of Jesus, to prison and to death.

WHILE HE WAS BLESSING THEM, HE WITHDREW FROM THEM AND WAS CARRIED UP INTO HEAVEN.

3. SEARCHING THE SCRIPTURES

In the first chapter of the Acts of the Apostles, Luke tells us that Jesus gave many "instructions through the Holy Spirit to the apostles" (1:2). There is the promise of a baptism with the Holy Spirit and the gift of power (1:5, 8). Also, they are to be his witnesses "in Jerusalem, in all Judea and Samaria, and to the ends of the earth" (1:8), which gives us a sketch of the travelogue that will be this second volume.

CONCLUSION:
JESUS, CONTEMPLATIVE IN ACTION

The program of the *Spiritual Exercises* concludes with the Ignatian ideal of finding God in all things, which is expressed in the "Contemplation to Attain the Love of God," that is, to grow in love of God. This calls for the effort to see how God dwells in everything: in the elements, in plants, in animals, in human beings, "and so in me" (paragraph 235). In response, it calls for surrendering oneself, and all that is most interior to oneself: memory, understanding, and will, to God. We are asked to go further and consider how God not only dwells in all things but "works and labors for me in all created things on the face of the earth" (paragraph 236). And so God is easy to find because God is everywhere; in every thing and in every situation, actively present and at work, and as though for me alone. This is not very different from what Paul says in his letter to the Romans (1:19–20), in reference to the Gentiles:

> For what can be known about God is plain to them, because God has shown it to them.

> Ever since the creation of the world his eternal power and divine nature, invisible though they are, have been understood and seen through the things he has made.

Prayer is also easy because it is really God who is doing the praying for us, as Paul says in this same letter:

> Likewise the Spirit helps us in our weakness; for we do not know how to pray as we ought, but that very Spirit intercedes with sighs too deep for words. (Rom 8:26)

Ignatius' aim in the *Exercises* is not to teach people how to pray, but to lead them into a deep union with the Triune God. It is by entering into the mind and heart of Jesus that we grow into this union and that we are drawn into the prayer of the Trinity.

At the end of the Gospel according to Luke, we leave the disciples of Jesus "continually in the temple blessing God" (24:53). They have walked and talked with Jesus, they have listened to his teachings on prayer, they have watched him go off alone to pray, and they have been with him as he prayed in their presence. They have seen him die on the cross, and they have shared in his post-resurrection appearances. They have come to believe in him as the Messiah, and they have worshiped him as he withdrew from them. They have learned not only about his prayer but also about his love. It is this love that fills them with joy and draws them into continual praise in the Temple as they await the coming of the Holy Spirit upon them. Their prayer has already become Trinitarian. With the coming of the Spirit they will begin their mission.

What Ignatius grasped in the gospels, and perhaps especially in the Gospel of Luke, is that Jesus is the way—open and accessible to all. It is through coming to know and love this man Jesus, both human and divine—to love him in his earthly life and in his risen life, and especially in his humanity—that we are drawn into union with God. By showing us something of Jesus' own prayer, Luke has revealed for every disciple a way into the mind and heart of Jesus.

Luke also reveals something of Jesus himself that seems to be at the center of the Ignatian ideal—an ideal that was later formulated by others as "contemplation in action." To be *at one and the same time* both contemplative and active is to emulate Jesus, who not only withdrew into solitude and prayer before entering into times of decision and action, but who never ceased to be in communion with the Father, even in the midst of action. This is why his prayer could be at once ecstatic and humble, joyful and shameless, carefree and grateful, childlike and silent, but always and everywhere unceasing. This is what it means to be a "contemplative in action": to become more and more one with Jesus in the mystery of *his* contemplation.

It means finally to rejoice with him in taking up the mission that he first announced in the synagogue at Nazareth:

> The Spirit of the Lord is upon me,
>
> because he has anointed me
>
> to bring good news to the poor. (4:18)

The most effective way for any of us to engage with him in his mission is to carry it out in continuing communion with the Father, through Jesus, and in the Holy Spirit.

ERIC JENSEN, S.J., a member of the Society of Jesus, received an MA in English from St. Louis University and studied Theology at Regis College in Toronto, where he was ordained to the ministerial priesthood in 1969. He was a high school teacher both before and after joining the Jesuits, and served as pastor of St. Ignatius Church in Winnipeg, Manitoba for ten years. He now leads retreats based on the *Spiritual Exercises of St. Ignatius* at Loyola House in Guelph, Ontario, where he also resides.